TO:

_____

FROM:

_____

DATE:

_____

Advent

THE STORY
of CHRISTMAS

SHERRI GRAGG

LIVE YOUR FAITH

Advent: The Story of Christmas
Copyright © 2019 by Sherri Gragg
First Edition, November 2019

Published by:

P.O. Box 1010
Siloam Springs, AR 72761
dayspring.com

Unless otherwise noted, all Scripture quotations are taken from THE HOLY
BIBLE, NEW INTERNATIONAL VERSION®, NIV® Copyright © 1973, 1978, 1984,
2011 by Biblica, Inc.® Used by permission. All rights reserved worldwide.

Scripture quotations marked ESV are taken from the ESV Bible® (The Holy
Bible, English Standard Version®) copyright ©2001 by Crossway Bibles, a
publishing ministry of Good News Publishers. Used by permission. All rights
reserved.

Scripture quotations marked THE MESSAGE are taken from THE MESSAGE,
copyright © 1993, 1994, 1995, 1996, 2000, 2001, 2002 by Eugene H. Peterson.
Used by permission of NavPress. All rights reserved. Represented by Tyndale
House Publishers, Inc.

Scripture quotations marked NKJV are taken from the New King James Ver-
sion®. Copyright © 1982 by Thomas Nelson. Used by permission. All rights
reserved.

Scripture quotations marked GNT are taken from the Good News Translation
in Today's English Version- Second Edition Copyright © 1992 by American
Bible Society. Used by Permission.

Scripture quotations marked NKJV are taken from the New King James Version. Copyright © 1982 by Thomas Nelson, Inc. Used by permission. All rights
reserved.

Written by: Sherri Gragg
Cover Design: Gearbox
Typeset Design: Greg Jackson of thinkpen.design

Printed in China
Prime: J1591
ISBN: 978-1-64454-440-2

Contents

A Note from the Author

My Friend,

I was sitting on a hillside in Israel when I first believed God loved me.

I spent a good portion of my early life in church. My mother tells me I attended my first service when I was no more than two weeks old. After that, I was there for Sunday school, Sunday morning worship, and Sunday evening worship as well. I was right back in the pew on Wednesday for our midweek "prayer meeting." During at least one week each year, I attended church every night of the week during our annual revival services. If I went to camp, it was church camp, where mid-morning chapel and evening services were daily requirements during the week.

So much church...

And yet, I somehow missed the message that God loved me. Instead, I became convinced that God was a harsh taskmaster who was ready to punish me at a moment's notice. God, I suspected, was disappointed in me even in my best moments and filled with burning wrath for me in my worst.

Just as the hobbits Frodo and Sam hid from the Eye of Mordor in J.R.R. Tolkien's *The Lord of the Rings,* I spent my childhood hiding from a terrifying, angry God.

As a teenager, I sank into the depths of despair. I thought about taking my life... a lot. One Sunday afternoon I could face my perceived worthlessness no longer. I dug through the bottom of the bathroom linen closet and found an old hard plastic box of razor blades. Then, I turned out the bathroom light and crawled into the shower to end my life.

But God foiled my plans.

No matter what I did, the box of razor blades would not open. Sobbing in fury, I stumbled from the shower and over to the toilet, where I slammed the box down onto the hard porcelain top of the tank over and over again in an attempt to break it open. It barely sustained a scratch.

Exhausted and utterly defeated, I threw the box into the bottom of the linen closet in disgust. I remember looking down at it as it lay in a tumble of old sheets and wornout bath towels and thinking that I couldn't do anything right, not even take my own life.

Then I looked down at my watch, wiped my tears, splashed some water on my face, and took a deep breath.

It was time for church. If I was late, I would pay for it.

After all, my father was the pastor.

Twenty years later, I found myself sitting on a hillside in Israel. An ancient stone wall was beneath me, a pale blue sky above me, and a lifetime of condemnation and shame was wrapped around my soul. A valley stretched out below me, soft and beautiful under the rays of the setting sun, as my guide and teacher, Dr. James Martin, read from a verse of Scripture that had always haunted me like no other.

"About three in the afternoon Jesus cried out in a loud voice, *"Eli, Eli, lema sabachthani?"* (which means "My God, my God, why have You forsaken me?"). Matthew 27:46 (NIV)

Even as a small child, I just couldn't understand it– How could God turn away from His only Son as He was suffering and dying on a Roman cross? If God could reject Jesus in a moment like that because He was too defiled with the sins of the world, *what hope was there for me?*

But Dr. Martin explained there was something else happening in that moment, something that was readily apparent to Jesus's followers when they heard Jesus's cry from the cross. There was a deeper truth at play that I, removed from the moment by infinite differences in culture and time, could not have imagined.

Dr. Martin explained that Jesus was using a well-known Semitic teaching device called a *remez*. A "remez" is a hint, a cue to look back and remember something one has already learned. In this case, Jesus was pointing His followers back to Psalm 22 by quoting the first verse of the Psalm.

Psalm 22 begins in despair, but it doesn't end there. After the Psalmist initial cry of, "My God, my God, why have You forsaken me?" he begins to remember that God has cared tenderly for him from the moment of his birth. Finally, in verse 24, he realizes his initial belief that God had forsaken him wasn't true at all—

> For He has not despised or scorned
> the suffering of the afflicted one;
> *he has not hidden His face from him*
> but has listened to his cry for help.
> (Psalm 22:24).

This is what Jesus was telling His disciples as He used a "remez" to point them to Psalm 22. In essence, He was saying, "Look, I know this looks bad. I know that as you watch me suffer and die it must seem like God has stepped out of the picture, but that isn't true! Remember Psalm 22? My God is right here with Me. He hasn't left Me in My suffering, not for one minute. He is so very near. So, My friends, have hope. This is not the end."

When Dr. Martin explained this, I thought, *Maybe I have had it all wrong. Maybe God does love me after all...*

This is what I hope you find in the pages of this book, my friend. In the years since I returned from Israel, I have eagerly researched the history, culture, and geography of the Bible. Through ancient Egyptian beliefs depicting Semitic people arriving in Egypt to buy grain during times of famine, I learned what Joseph's brothers' clothes, hair, and weapons looked like. The archeological discovery of tiny, beautifully preserved dioramas in the tomb of an Egyptian nobleman revealed what day-to-day life was like for the Israelites during the long years they suffered under the yoke of Egyptian slavery.

As I studied the migration of Abram and Sarai, I traced their most likely routes along maps of ancient roadways in Palestine and in the Fertile Crescent.

Sometimes, the things I discovered shocked me. Imagine my surprise when I realized that much of the information in the Christmas pageants of my childhood was drawn not from Scripture, but from Christian novels and traditional Christmas songs and stories.

There were days I spent wrestling with the stories I had always heard as they conflicted not only with cultural background, but sometimes the Scriptures themselves. For instance, I was told that Jesus was a two-year-old toddler when the wise men came to visit, but we know Mary and Joseph were far from their home in Nazareth—and Joseph's livelihood—when Jesus was born in Bethlehem. It would have been impractical and unreasonable for them to linger in Bethlehem for two years.

Additionally, Luke 2:39 clearly tells us that once Joseph and Mary had done everything required of them by Levitical law following Jesus's birth, they returned home to Nazareth. Mary and Jesus's time of purification would have been completed in weeks, not years. Even if we allow some additional time for Mary to fully recover from childbirth before making the long journey back to Nazareth, Jesus would have still been a baby when the wise men arrived.

The hours spent in research have been sweet ones for me, but I understand that not everyone enjoys reading archeological reports, or books on the culture and history of the Bible. This is why I have taken all I have learned and turned it into narrative. It is my hope that, by wrapping these truths in the power of story, you will discover that God loves you more than you ever imagined. This Advent season, we will journey together from Eden to Jerusalem, following the scarlet ribbon of God's great redemptive plan as it is drawn throughout the annals of history by ordinary men and women.

O Come, O Come, Emmanuel. Our hearts long for You...

Christ's Peace,
Sherri Gragg

Banished with a Plan

EVE   ABRAHAM

SURELY HE TOOK UP OUR PAIN
AND BORE OUR SUFFERING,
YET WE CONSIDERED HIM PUNISHED BY GOD,
STRICKEN BY HIM, AND AFFLICTED.
BUT HE WAS PIERCED FOR OUR TRANSGRESSIONS,
HE WAS CRUSHED FOR OUR INIQUITIES;
THE PUNISHMENT THAT BROUGHT
US PEACE WAS ON HIM,
AND BY HIS WOUNDS WE ARE HEALED.
WE ALL, LIKE SHEEP, HAVE GONE ASTRAY,
EACH OF US HAS TURNED TO OUR OWN WAY;
AND THE LORD HAS LAID ON HIM
THE INIQUITY OF US ALL.

ISAIAH 53:4–6

Eve lifted a trembling hand and placed it on her chest. Beneath her fingers she felt the racing of her heart. She took a deep breath, then reached to part the leaves of the fig tree so that she could see out into the garden. A cool evening breeze stirred her hiding place in the deep shadows of the tree line. Smooth, verdant paths wove through rows of fruit and nut trees. Pistachio shells blushed pink against clusters of teardrop-shaped leaves. Tall date palms, heavily laden with golden fruit, towered over cascades of colorful flowers. Violet crocuses, sweet-scented roses, and pale hollyhocks would soon glow underneath the light of the moon after the last rays of sun faded. A stream flowed through the center of the garden, babbling and leaping over stones as it rushed toward its longed-for destination: the clear, cool lake that bordered the southern edge of the desert oasis.

This evening the garden looked the same as any other night, and yet…it wasn't. Eve felt uneasy as she watched a small doe creep to the edge of the stream for a drink. It hesitated, then froze for a moment, perfectly still, before finally bending low to drink. A bird's harsh cry pierced the stillness, and the startled doe bolted into the trees with eyes widened with terror.

Then the garden was once again unnaturally still, as if the earth itself was holding its breath.

Eve's heart raced faster. Instinctively, she turned to reach for Adam, but when her eyes met his, her hand dropped, and she backed away. She saw her own terror reflected in his eyes, but there was something else there too. In the eyes that had always met hers with tenderness and delight, there was…anger. And blame. Yes, blame. Eve's face flushed hot with guilt. Self-consciously, she tugged at the garment of fig leaves she had hastily tied together, stem to stem. They covered her body, but they felt too short, too thin, too fragile to cover her shame. Eve wrapped her arms around herself, hung her head, and squeezed her eyes shut tight. Tears spilled between her lashes before silently slipping down her cheeks and dropping softly to the earth beneath her.

Suddenly the silence of the garden was broken.

"Where are you?"

The voice rolled like deep thunder, but there was music in it too. Eve uttered a small cry and drew further into the shadows. For a long moment, the silence of the garden hung weighty and breathless as the Creator awaited His children's reply.

Adam drew a shuddering breath, parted the leaves of the fig tree, and stepped out of the shadows to face his Lord. In despair, Eve realized that hiding was futile. It always had been. How could the morning hide from the rising sun? How could the darkness of the shadows ever resist the brilliance of the Creator's light?

Then Adam spoke, his voice trembling. "I heard You in the garden, and I was afraid because I was naked; so I hid" (Genesis 3:10).

Adam and Eve lifted their eyes to meet their Creator's and found deep sadness there. *"Who told you you were naked?"* He asked them. *"Did you eat from that tree I told you not to eat from?"* (3:11 THE MESSAGE)

"The Woman You gave me as a companion, she gave me fruit from the tree, and yes, I ate it" (3:12 THE MESSAGE).

God turned to Eve, and His voice was filled with pity and heavy with sorrow. *"What is this you have done?"*

Eve began to weep. "The serpent seduced me," she said, "and I ate" (3:13 THE MESSAGE).

A cold, sinister laugh came from a nearby pomegranate tree where an emerald-green python lay curled in its branches. The serpent was unlike any of the other animals in the garden. It was lovelier, more graceful...and cunning. Its golden eyes glowed with intelligence.

Inch by inch, the serpent unwound its body and began its long, slow spiral descent to the ground. When it reached the garden floor, it rose up to its full height and glided across the grass to join them.

"Because you've done this, you're cursed," God said to Adam, "cursed beyond all cattle and wild animals, cursed to slink on your belly and eat dirt all your life. I'm declaring war between you and the Woman, between your offspring and hers" (3:14–15 THE MESSAGE).

But the curse extended far beyond the deception of the serpent. Eve's heart broke as God explained the consequences of His children's choice. From that moment on, the wound of sin would fracture their relationships and fill their lives with fear, pain, and struggle. Eons of famine, war, and bloodshed would stalk their descendants. No corner of the earth was spared the curse of sin.

Adam and Eve were banished from their garden home. Their bleak future lay beyond the gates of Eden, and there in the wilderness, they would die.

As the first evening star rose on the horizon, Adam and Eve took one last walk with their Creator. Step by silent, sorrowful step, they made their way to the gates of Eden. When they reached the entrance, they stood at the threshold gazing out at the barren landscape of their future home. A cold wind blew Eve's hair off her face and dried her tears as they trickled down her cheeks. Adam took her hand, and they began to exit through the gates. Eve held tight to the merciful promise of the Creator that, though she and Adam had betrayed Him, He would someday redeem their separation and bring them home again. He would make a way to bridge the chasm of sin and death with a holy sacrifice of love.

One day, God's own Son would be born, and that child, the last Adam, would end the curse, reconcile His children, and bring them home. As Eve took step after step away from Eden and into the cold, black night, she clung to the promise that it was not the end. God would make a way.

Creator of all,

Like my mother, Eve, my heart is weak with rebellion. I too have been deceived and hidden in the shadows, lost and afraid, as You longingly called my name. My way has been marked with pain and salted with the grief of my tears. My sin has made me weak and left me broken.

Give me the strength to cling to Your promise of redemption on the days Eden's gates close fast behind me and the sin-marred wilderness stretches before me. I cast myself at the feet of Your mercy and grace. Let the promise of Your redemption this Advent season carry me into new life and an undying hope for tomorrow.

Amen

A Call
and a
Promise

EVE

ABRAHAM

JOSEPH

BY FAITH ABRAHAM,
WHEN CALLED TO GO TO A PLACE HE WOULD
LATER RECEIVE AS HIS INHERITANCE,
OBEYED AND WENT,
EVEN THOUGH HE DID NOT KNOW
WHERE HE WAS GOING.

HEBREWS 11:8

The morning sun was already hot on Abram's back as he gave one last sharp tug on the strap securing Sarai's pack to her donkey. He then turned to look up into his wife's beautiful, dark eyes fringed with thick lashes. She offered him a small smile and extended her hand to him, which he squeezed reassuringly before turning back to make one last sweep through their home to be sure they had packed up everything.

The moment he stepped through the door, the temperature dropped dramatically. Years before, when Abram had first arrived in Haran with his aging father and extended family, he was stunned by the rows of "beehive" homes clustered together along the banks of the Balikh River. The odd structures were brilliant adaptations to life in the scorching heat. Each room of these homes was constructed of mud, straw, and stone and topped with a lofty cone roof left open at the top. The heat rose up and out, creating a cool and comfortable shelter year round.

The homes were easily expanded as a family grew. One wall was simply knocked out, a new beehive structure built, and an arched doorway constructed to join them. Abram walked from room to room, his footsteps echoing in the barren space. Walls once hung with colorful textiles were now spotless. Floors once draped in bright rugs and strewn with pillows were swept clean.

He reached the last room and stood silently in the doorway, watching as motes of dust danced in the beam of sunlight falling from the roof-opening above. He turned to place his forehead against the cool wall and took a deep breath.

Empty.

He was trading the abundance and security of prosperous Haran for miles and miles of empty. Empty stomachs. Empty water skins. His now-empty home for life in a tent. Who in his right mind would take his family, servants, and all he possessed into a world of empty and unknowns?

Abram placed one rough hand against the smooth, cool adobe and looked up to gaze through the opening of the roof and into a clear blue sky. And there, into the emptiness, he repeated the promise of God:

> *Go from your country, your people*
> *and your father's household to the land I will show you.*
> *I will make you into a great nation,*
> *and I will bless you;*
> *I will make your name great,*
> *and you will be a blessing.*
> *I will bless those who bless you,*
> *and whoever curses you I will curse;*
> *and all peoples on earth*
> *will be blessed through you.*
> Genesis 12:1–3

Canaan was a land empty of guarantees, and yet it overflowed with something infinitely better: God's promises. Abram was risking everything to grasp hold of God's promises with a heart filled with audacious faith.

Moments later, when Abram stepped back across his threshold for the last time, the heat hit him like a wall, shimmering off of the ground beneath his feet and stealing his breath. In the distance, the Balikh River danced in the sunlight, a glistening jewel set into the verdant abundance of the Fertile Crescent. He walked back to Sarai, turned his eyes toward Canaan, and with a shout to his men to move out, took his first steps westward toward the land of promise.

Yahweh-Yireh (The Lord Will Provide),

Abram traded the abundance and security of Haran for the promise that You would fill the more desperately empty places in his life:

his longing for a purpose

a land to call his own

his desperate, aching yearning for a child

I find myself driven to make my home in the land of proofs and measures, commodities and securities. But, as with Abram, You call me to journey with You into the land of promise. Help me remember, my God, that the "guarantees" of this world are an illusion; they are shaky ground upon which to build my life. As I wait for You this Advent, may I courageously embrace Your promises that never fail.

Amen

Count the Stars

EVE   ABRAHAM   JOSEPH

BY FAITH EVEN SARAH, WHO WAS
PAST CHILDBEARING AGE,
WAS ENABLED TO BEAR CHILDREN
BECAUSE SHE CONSIDERED HIM FAITHFUL
WHO HAD MADE THE PROMISE.
AND SO FROM THIS ONE MAN, AND
HE AS GOOD AS DEAD,
CAME DESCENDANTS AS NUMEROUS
AS THE STARS IN THE SKY
AND AS COUNTLESS AS THE SAND
ON THE SEASHORE.
HEBREWS 11:11–12

Abram lay on his mat, listening to the sounds of the night—the snoring of his men, the intermittent scurrying of tiny rodent feet along the edge of the tent, the rhythmic rise and fall of calls from countless nocturnal birds. He rolled over with a groan, searching and failing to find some kind of relief for his aching back.

He was getting too old for life in a tent. He was surrounded by goatskin walls instead of stone or adobe. The mats on the floor offered precious little cushion for ever-stiffening joints and muscles. The routine was daily and predictable: pack up, move to a new plot of ground for the herds and flocks, struggle to find water, pitch your tent, and then get up the next day and do it all again.

Abram heard a familiar cough as Sarai stirred on the other side of the tent in the women's room. He pictured her there, awake too, staring at the thin line of pale moonlight creeping under the bottom edge of the tent as her heart strained to find a remaining glimmer of hope in the dark night of God's long-delayed promises. Aching back, empty womb, broken heart.

Abram had asked her to give up her family, her country, and every comfort of home to wander Canaan with him. If she did, he told her, God would finally give her the child for which she had so longed. Abram believed God, and Sarai believed Abram. But now, the years stretched out behind them, ticking away until all hope for a child was almost lost.

They were old now, so very old. God's promise and Abram's faith had grown dim.

Abram sighed, his eyes fluttered closed, and the tent grew silent. And then, Abram heard the voice of God, soft and so very near.

"Do not be afraid, Abram. I am your shield, your very great reward" (Genesis 15:1).

Tears filled the old man's eyes as he cried out into the darkness, "Sovereign LORD, what can You give me since I remain childless…? You have given me no children, so a servant in my household will be my heir" (15:2–3).

God responded to Abram's doubt, his questioning and accusation with remarkable tenderness. *"This man will not be your heir, but a son who is your own flesh and blood will be your heir"* (15:4). Then, God took Abram from his tent and out into the night, bright with starlight. Abram pulled his cloak closer against the chill.

"Look up at the sky and count the stars," God said to him, *"if indeed you can count them. So shall your offspring be"* (15:5).

Abram lifted his deeply lined face to the sky, strewn with a multitude of stars, each crafted by God's own hand. He gasped at the magnitude of it, in awe of a sky laden with riotous wonder, the handicraft of a God who specializes in the impossible.

And Abram believed.

More than three decades later, Abram, now renamed Abraham by God, paced back and forth in front of his tent as the sounds of Sarah's cries mingled with the songs of the night.

And then, a baby's thin cry abruptly joined the chorus of creation.

Abraham cried out in joy and fell to his knees in worship of a God who was faithful to His promises, a God for whom nothing is impossible. Moments later, a servant knelt beside him and placed Abraham's swaddled newborn son in his ancient father's arms. Abraham bent his head low to brush the top of the baby's head with his lips.

So tiny, so small, so fragile—a promise fulfilled just in time. Abraham turned his face to the heavens, where a multitude of stars stretched out into infinity.

And Abraham believed.

Emmanuel,

Oh, how we long for You. Our hearts are broken, our faith worn thin as we wait for the promise of Your deliverance. Come tenderly to us, as You did to Abraham. Let our ears be filled with Your words of comfort and peace, our eyes awestruck by Your handiwork in creation. Renew our faith, our courage, our strength.

We wait for You and believe.

Amen

Here Comes the Dreamer

ABRAHAM · JOSEPH · MOSES

BECAUSE THE PATRIARCHS
WERE JEALOUS OF JOSEPH,
THEY SOLD HIM AS A SLAVE INTO EGYPT.
BUT GOD WAS WITH HIM
AND RESCUED HIM FROM ALL HIS TROUBLES.
HE GAVE JOSEPH WISDOM
AND ENABLED HIM TO GAIN THE GOODWILL
OF PHARAOH KING OF EGYPT.
SO PHARAOH MADE HIM RULER OVER EGYPT
AND ALL HIS PALACE.
ACTS 7:9–10

Here comes the Dreamer," Simeon said in disgust.

Reuben squinted into the glare of the midday sun as it reflected off of the rocky landscape. In the distance a figure approached with a brightly colored cloak of red, blue, and gold flapping in the breeze.

It was the patriarchal coat that, according to custom, signified the authority of the firstborn son. As the oldest of twelve brothers, it should have been forty-two-year-old Reuben's coat. Instead, it graced the frame of the awkward teenage boy who was eleventh in line, the favorite son of a favorite wife. Once again, Reuben was reminded of the harsh truth he had faced every day for the past seventeen years.

His father loved young Joseph best.

Reuben surveyed his brothers as each of them trained cold, angry eyes on the boy in the distance. Jacob's favoritism of Joseph had always been difficult to take, and lately Joseph had done nothing to help the situation. First, he gave their father an unfavorable report concerning his brothers' care of the sheep. Then, he informed the entire family that he had two dreams in which his brothers, and even his father, would one day bow down to him. Reuben knew it was only a matter of time until long-simmering resentments finally boiled over.

Reuben was stirred out of his reverie by the motion of Levi's approach, with one hand grasping the hilt of his sword so tightly his knuckles were white. When he spoke, his voice was low and calculated.

"Let's kill him," Levi said, his nostrils flaring. He then jabbed his sword in the direction of a nearby cistern, where a three-foot-wide opening led to a dark, manmade cavern, fifteen feet deep.

"We can throw him into one of these cisterns and say an animal got him. Then we will see what happens to his dreams."

The brothers all laughed in agreement. For a moment, Reuben imagined what it would be like to finally be free of Joseph. Perhaps then his father, Jacob, would allow him his rightful honor as the eldest son. But at what cost? What would become of Jacob if he lost his precious son Joseph?

"No," said Reuben. "Just throw him into the cistern. Don't hurt him."

One by one the brothers, burly warriors, stood to their feet.

Joseph kicked a stone ahead of him, stirring up small swirls of dust on the dry ground. He heard the bleating of sheep and looked up to see his brothers gathered together as they awaited his arrival. He smiled, raised a hand in greeting, and then slowly lowered it again as he saw their clenched jaws, hard eyes, and balled fists.

Joseph's heart beat faster. He took a few more slow steps and stopped. Then, in a hopeless attempt to save himself, he turned to run away. But he was too slow, too late. Strong arms wrapped around his waist as rough hands gripped his ankles and wrists, and ripped his coat from his back. He twisted and kicked in terror, but he was no match for his powerful brothers. A moment later he fell down, down, down, through the darkness, and crashed onto the stone floor below.

After a moment, Joseph struggled to his feet. His eyes were wide with terror, his face flushed in pain. Bright sunlight and harsh laughter fell through the opening far above him.

"Let me out!" he cried. "Let me out! Please...please don't leave me down here. Please don't leave me..."

Joseph drew a ragged breath and wiped his eyes with the back of his hand. Tenderly, he touched his face just above his left eye, and when he brought his fingers away, they were covered in blood. He paced the floor of the cistern, his eyes never leaving the opening above. Then he sobbed in despair, sat down on the floor, and rested his back against the wall. He pulled his knees to his chest, wrapped his arms around them, and lay his forehead on the tops of his knees.

Far above, he could hear his older brothers laughing and joking as they passed around water skins and loaves of bread for their noonday meal. Joseph had always been in awe of them. Some of his earliest memories were of him toddling after them when they were teenagers. As a boy, he had begged them to take him along when they went out with the sheep. As an adolescent, he had watched carefully as they polished their swords and packed their bags in preparation to drive the sheep to greener pastures. But anytime he drew near to his brothers, rough hands shoved him away. In recent months, they could no longer even speak decently to him. Joseph's brothers hated him.

Bloodied and bruised, he finally realized just how deep that hatred ran.

Suddenly the jovial sound of his brothers' comaraderie was interrupted by the unmistakable sounds of a caravan. The clip-clop of donkey hooves mingled with the rough voices of the traders as they called to one another. The hard clink of slaves' shackles was punctuated by the crack of a whip and the deep, guttural groans of camels laden with heavy bundles of spices.

"Brothers," said Judah, "what are we going to get out of killing our brother and concealing the evidence? Let's sell him to the Ishmaelites, but let's not kill him—he is, after all, our brother, our own flesh and blood" (Genesis 37:26–27 THE MESSAGE).

A murmur of assent reached Joseph. A moment later, a long rope dropped down into the cistern. Joseph's heartbeat pounded in his ears as he stood to his feet and reached for the rope. Then, with trembling hands, he grasped it. The moment he shoved his foot into the loop at the bottom, it grew taut and he began his ascent out of the cistern.

As soon as he reached the top, his brothers seized him and shoved him to the ground in front of one of the traders. Joseph struggled to his feet and stood trembling as the trader circled him, inspecting him carefully. The trader cast a critical stare at the gash above Joseph's eye before grasping him by the chin, prying open his mouth, and inspecting his teeth. Then he stepped back, nodded in satisfaction, reached into his money pouch, and pulled out a handful of coins. Joseph watched in horror as the man counted twenty pieces of silver into Judah's palm. The moment the last coin fell, heavy iron shackles fell around Joseph's neck and around his wrists. He looked down in disbelief as one of the traders secured his chains to the camel in front of him. Then the trader called out to his companions, the camel lurched forward, and Joseph took his first steps toward Egypt.

Joseph cast one last glance over his shoulder as his brothers faded into the life he was forever leaving behind. Judah, still as stone, stared at him while his other brothers laughed and tossed a loose ball back and forth. Suddenly, a breeze caught the object and unfurled a garment of red, blue, and gold.

Judah had saved Joseph's life, but it was a cruel deliverance. The favored son had become a slave.

Almighty God,

You have promised that light dawns in the darkness for Your children. When my heart sinks under the weight of heartbreak and despair, remind me that You are not finished. Betrayal doesn't have the last word. Lives swept away by loss may yet be restored. Because of Your great love, my darkest night is merely the stage for the brilliant Star of Bethlehem.

Amen

(Prayer inspired by Psalm 112:4)

All for the Good

ABRAHAM — JOSEPH — MOSES

34

THEN A FAMINE STRUCK
ALL EGYPT AND CANAAN,
BRINGING GREAT SUFFERING,
AND OUR ANCESTORS COULD NOT FIND FOOD.
WHEN JACOB HEARD THAT
THERE WAS GRAIN IN EGYPT,
HE SENT OUR FOREFATHERS ON THEIR FIRST VISIT.
ON THEIR SECOND VISIT,
JOSEPH TOLD HIS BROTHERS WHO HE WAS,
AND PHARAOH LEARNED ABOUT JOSEPH'S FAMILY.
AFTER THIS, JOSEPH SENT FOR HIS FATHER JACOB
AND HIS WHOLE FAMILY, SEVENTY-FIVE IN ALL.
THEN JACOB WENT DOWN TO EGYPT,
WHERE HE AND OUR ANCESTORS DIED.

ACTS 7:11–15

Joseph sat on a low, ornately painted bench on the veranda of his home. It faced a walled garden bordered with sycamore fig trees. A row of columns, intricately painted in turquoise, yellow, and red, lined the edge of the veranda, framing the view.

From upstairs, Joseph heard his wife, Asenath, call to their sons. The boys' laughter and the sound of their bare feet running to their mother floated down into the portico below, then faded away.

Deep in the shadows, Joseph's servants watched their Hebrew master warily. They were accustomed to the demands of serving such a powerful man, but this day something was different. First, the home had been filled with foreigners who bought grain and then inexplicably stayed for a feast. Then, after Joseph released the men to begin their journey home, he ordered the servants to secretly put the foreigners' payment pouches of silver, and the master's personal silver cup, into their bags of grain. Once the men had time to journey a short distance out of the city, the servants were to bring them back under the charge of theft.

Now Joseph waited, lost in thought, his face creased with sorrow.

Joseph lifted his right hand to lightly run his fingers across the gold chain around his neck, a gift from Pharaoh on the day he had named him governor of all of Egypt. As he did, light shimmered off a large oval ring on his finger, the signet ring of Pharaoh himself.

Joseph was the picture of Egyptian nobility—clean shaven, eyes heavily lined with kohl, and eyelids painted blue. His shoulder-length dark hair was combed back and tucked behind his ears, pushing them forward to portray the Egyptian ideal of beauty.

But beneath his tunic of the finest linen beat the heart of the great-great-grandson of Abraham. Joseph was a child of God's promise, living in a foreign land.

Joseph's mind wandered back through his years in Egypt, the

"land of his suffering" (Genesis 41:52). For the past nine years, he had been the most powerful man in all the land, second only to Pharaoh. During that time, he had accumulated wealth, married the daughter of Potiphera, the priest of On, and had two sons. Through his careful administration and God's guiding, he had saved Egypt from a fierce famine.

But before that, he had been both a prisoner and a slave, sold into captivity by his own brothers. He was only a boy when they stripped his coat from his back and threw him in a cistern to die. His brother Judah saved his life when he suggested they sell him to a caravan of Ishmaelite traders. It had been the darkest, most hopeless day of Joseph's life, and now, as he looked back on it, he struggled to reconcile the ugly and painful truth the past events had revealed: the loss of everything and everyone he knew and loved, the sting of a slave master's whip, the humiliation of the auction block, the countless tears of despair on a dungeon floor... It all felt meaningless, yet it was all part of God's plan. He was there in the middle of it, redeeming Joseph's suffering to save the line of Abraham.

"Master..."

The voice of Joseph's steward broke through the silence. Joseph turned to his left, where the trusted servant stood waiting in the doorway.

"Show them in," Joseph said.

The steward stepped to the side, and one by one Joseph's brothers filed into the room. Reuben, the eldest, led the way. Benjamin, the youngest, brought up the rear. Trembling, they fell to their knees before Joseph and pressed their foreheads to the ground.

What would they do once they knew the Egyptian ruler sitting before them, holding their lives in his hands, was the brother they had sold into slavery and assumed dead? Would they accept him at last? Could he, Joseph, ever forgive them?

Joseph decided to hold onto his anonymity for just a moment longer.

"What is this you have done?" Joseph demanded of his brothers (44:15).

"What can we say to my lord?" Judah replied. "What can we say? How can we prove our innocence? God has uncovered your servants' guilt. We are now my lord's slaves—we ourselves and the one who was found to have the cup" (44:16).

"Far be it from me to do such a thing!" Joseph said. "Only the man who was found to have the cup will become my slave. The rest of you, go back to your father in peace" (44:17).

Judah stepped forward and began to beg for the life of his youngest brother, Benjamin, whose sack had held the silver cup. His words tumbled out in a rush of grief, sorrow, and the weight of regret.

"We have an aged father. If my father, whose life is closely bound up with the boy's life, sees that the boy isn't there, he will die. Please let your servant remain here as my lord's slave in place of the boy" (44:20, 30–31, 33).

Joseph could bear it no more.

"Have everyone leave my presence!" he shouted to his servants (45:1).

They scurried from the room, leaving Joseph alone with his brothers. He stood, covered his face with his hands, and began to weep. Years of loneliness, loss, and rejection washed over him. He wrapped his arms around himself and bent double, wailing, as his terrified brothers huddled together. When Joseph's tears were spent, he stood to look at them and, between ragged breaths, reached across infinite loss to find it miraculously redeemed by a merciful and faithful God.

"I am Joseph!" he said. "Is my father still living?" (45:3)

His brothers stared wide-eyed at him, their hearts pounding, mute with terror.

"Come close to me," Joseph whispered (45:4).

Judah and Reuben led the way, tears in their eyes, as the brothers crossed the room toward Joseph.

"I am Joseph your brother whom you sold into Egypt," Joseph said. "But don't feel badly, don't blame yourselves for selling me. God was behind it…. God sent me on ahead to pave the way and make sure there was a remnant in the land, to save your lives in an amazing act of deliverance. So you see, it wasn't you who sent me here but God" (45:4–8 THE MESSAGE).

Reuben placed a hand on each of Joseph's shoulders, his eyes searching his younger brother's face in disbelief. Judah collapsed to his knees, covered his face with his hands, and began to sob. One by one, the other brothers surrounded Joseph as stunned silence gave way to shouts of joy and tears of gratitude.

Gradually, the room grew quiet as the brothers stepped aside to make way for Benjamin, Joseph's younger brother and the only other child of his mother, Rachel. Joseph wrapped his arms around Benjamin. Tears slipped down the other brothers' faces as they stood silently watching Benjamin and Joseph cling to each other and weep.

The brothers soon left for Canaan once more, but this time with hearts filled with joy, for behind them they pulled empty carts and wagons, supplied by Pharaoh, to bring their father, wives, and children back to Egypt. There, God would fulfill another of His promises to Abraham. In the abundance of Egypt, Abraham's descendants would flourish until they numbered the grains of sand and the stars in the sky and become a mighty nation from which God would bring forth the Redeemer of all creation.

Merciful and faithful God,

There is no harm that comes our way that is beyond Your ability to redeem. Through the life of a slave boy betrayed by his own brothers, You preserved the children of Abraham and the line of the Messiah. When my heart is broken by betrayal, help me to follow Joseph's example and look not at the hand of the one who has wounded me, but to Your hand that redeems and heals all. Then, I will sing of the mighty works that You have done.

Amen

Abundance in Bondage

JOSEPH   MOSES   BALAAM

AS THE TIME DREW NEAR FOR GOD TO
FULFILL HIS PROMISE TO ABRAHAM,
THE NUMBER OF OUR PEOPLE IN EGYPT
HAD GREATLY INCREASED.
THEN "A NEW KING, TO WHOM JOSEPH MEANT
NOTHING, CAME TO POWER IN EGYPT."
HE DEALT TREACHEROUSLY WITH OUR PEOPLE
AND OPPRESSED OUR ANCESTORS
BY FORCING THEM TO THROW
OUT THEIR NEWBORN BABIES
SO THAT THEY WOULD DIE.
AT THAT TIME MOSES WAS BORN,
AND HE WAS NO ORDINARY CHILD.
FOR THREE MONTHS HE WAS
CARED FOR BY HIS FAMILY.
WHEN HE WAS PLACED OUTSIDE,
PHARAOH'S DAUGHTER TOOK HIM
AND BROUGHT HIM UP AS HER OWN SON.
ACTS 7:17–21

Jochebed gasped for breath and leaned her head back against Puah, the midwife who was supporting her as she crouched on the birthing stool.

"Just one more push, Jochebed, and your baby will be here," said Shiphrah. The second midwife crouched in front of her, preparing to receive the baby.

A wave of pain swept over Jochebed as the next contraction began. Then, with one last cry, she brought her baby into the world. Shiphrah gently laid the baby on his mother's chest.

"Is it a boy or a girl?" Jochebed asked as her eyes anxiously searched Shiphrah's face for the answer.

"God has blessed you with a son," she said softly as she helped adjust the newborn so he could nurse.

"No, no, no!" Jochebed cried. She wrapped her arms around her baby boy as if, somehow, she could protect him from Pharaoh's latest cruel solution to what he considered an Israelite overpopulation problem. First he had enslaved them, but when they continued to flourish despite backbreaking labor, Pharaoh ordered every Israelite baby boy thrown in the Nile.

"My son, my son," Jochebed wept.

Puah held the new mother close and stroked her hair as Shiphrah placed a blanket over mother and infant. Jochebed lifted a weary, trembling hand to caress her baby's dark hair. Slowly, his eyes fluttered closed. She tenderly lifted his hand and he instinctively wrapped his tiny fingers around hers. He was so strong, beautiful, perfect in every way.

She would hide him for as long as she could.

Jochebed lifted the papyrus basket onto the table and studied it for a moment before thrusting a small wooden spatula into a jar of pitch. As her daughter, Miriam, watched closely, Jochebed began to coat the basket with the pitch to make it waterproof. After a moment, she paused in her work to look down at the chubby three-month-old baby strapped to her chest. He looked up at his mother and smiled. She laughed softly and bent to kiss the top of his head as her eyes filled with tears. She had hidden him for as long as she could. He was growing too big, his cry too strong. It was only a matter of time before soldiers, or even their Egyptian neighbors, discovered him. If her baby boy was destined for the Nile, she would give him the only chance she could. She would tuck him into a little basket boat, whisper a prayer, and set it afloat in the reeds. Perhaps, somehow, he would be saved.

The next morning, just as the sun painted a thin golden line across the horizon, Jochebed finished nursing her baby for the last time. Gently, she lifted him to her shoulder and felt his warm cheek nuzzle into the side of her neck. As silent tears began to run down her face, she walked to the table to place him in the basket. She bent low to kiss his forehead and then tucked his blanket around him. She placed the lid on the basket, hoisted it to her hip, and then began the short walk to the Nile.

Once she reached the shore, Jochebed waded out into the water and gently set the basket afloat among the reeds. As she stood, the lithe movement of a crocodile, slipping beneath the water on the opposite bank, caught her eye. She looked back at the little boat basket in the reeds that sheltered her fragile baby boy. If, by some miracle, he was not found by an Egyptian fisherman and tossed into the depths of the Nile with so many other Israelite baby boys, he was almost doomed to become prey for the deadly wildlife that dwelt there.

She had given him all she could for as long as she could, but she knew it was foolish to even dream of his deliverance.

With empty arms and a heavy heart, she turned toward home.

Jochebed, absorbed in her grief, had not noticed that Miriam had slipped from her bed and followed her mother to the river. Now the child crouched in the reeds, watching to see what fate would befall her little brother. She sat very still as the sun rose higher and the river fell into the early-morning rhythms of daybreak. All around her, bright birds, their wings like jewels, flitted from reed to reed searching for food. A family of hippos splashed into the water downriver, startling a large white ibis into flight. It passed overhead, so close that she could see its bright black eye and hear the sound of its powerful wings whooshing the air.

And then, the sound of voices reached her.

Miriam held her breath as one of Pharaoh's daughters and her maidens approached the edge of the water. The princess sat down on the shore, closed her eyes, and turned her face to the rising sun. The sound of the maiden's voices began to fade away as they moved farther down the shore, and then the quiet was pierced by a baby's cry.

Miriam held her breath as she watched the princess scan the shore, searching for the sound. After a moment, her eyes fell on the basket in the reeds. Miriam's heart pounded as the princess called to her maidens, ordering them to bring her the basket. One of the women waded into the reeds, grasped the edge of the home-made boat, and tugged it along behind her until it rested in front of the princess.

Carefully, she opened the basket and the crying grew louder. She reached into the basket and tenderly lifted the baby to her shoulder, gently rocking him back and forth.

"This must be one of the Hebrew babies," she said softly (Exodus 2:6 THE MESSAGE).

Miriam bounded from the reeds and raced along the shore to stand before the princess. "Do you want me to go and get a nursing mother from the Hebrews so she can nurse the baby for you?" she asked (2:7 THE MESSAGE).

"Yes, go!" the princess replied.

A few moments later, Miriam was back before the princess, her own mother beside her. Gently, Pharaoh's daughter laid the baby in her arms. "Take him," she said. "Nurse him and I will pay you. When he is weaned, bring him to me and I will raise him as my son."

Jochebed nodded, stunned beyond speech, and turned to take her baby back home.

For the next four years, Jochebed nursed her son, and as she did, she whispered precious truths over him that would shape the future of not only his life but the lives of all Israel.

"You are the son of Levi," she said, "the son of Abraham, Isaac, and Jacob. We are a people of promise..."

The day the boy turned four years old, Jochebed knelt before him and tied a linen kilt around his waist. She held him close to her chest for a moment and then kissed his forehead. Then she took him by the hand and led him out of the house and down the streets of the city. Together they walked past butcher shops and granaries, past women weaving cloth and men pressing a mixture of earth and straw into molds to make bricks.

When they walked beneath the pylons of the temple and past a long line of ram-headed sphinxes, the boy's eyes grew wide as he gripped his mother's hand tighter. A moment later, they stood before the palace guards.

"I have the princess's son," Jochebed said.

One of the men turned and spoke to a nearby servant, who then walked quickly into the recesses of the entry hall and disappeared into the shadows. When he returned, the princess was with him. The boy stared wide-eyed at the woman before him. Her long, straight hair was held back by a golden headpiece. A linen tunic, secured at one shoulder, fell below her knees. A wide-banded necklace of gold and turquoise lay across her collarbone. Her eyes were heavily lined with kohl, her eyelids painted blue, her lips stained red.

She smiled at Jochebed, then knelt in front of the child.

"I will name him Moses," she said, "because I drew him out of the water."

Moses looked up at Jochebed. She smiled reassuringly at him and then gently placed his hand in the hand of the princess. She stood watching for a moment as the pair disappeared beneath ornate lotus flower columns and Moses took the first steps into his new life.

But Moses was also taking his first steps into God's plan for him. For the one whom the princess "drew out of the water" would one day deliver his entire nation from Egyptian oppression by God's mighty hand. Moses, the son of Levi, Abraham, Isaac, and Jacob, was destined to lead Israel to God's promised land.

Wondrous Redeemer,

I thank You for each servant who has helped draw the scarlet cord of redemption through the halls of history. Through the faithfulness of two midwives, the fierce love of a mother, and the compassion of an Egyptian princess, You saved the life of Moses. Moses then led Your people out of bondage, preserving the line of Your Son, Jesus.

Jesus came to set the captives free. Grant me enduring faithfulness, fierce love, and unwavering compassion today as I continue to work alongside You to bring Your good kingdom to earth.

Amen

Lamb of God

JOSEPH   MOSES   BALAAM

FOR THE LAMB AT THE CENTER OF THE
THRONE WILL BE THEIR SHEPHERD;
"HE WILL LEAD THEM
TO SPRINGS OF LIVING WATER."
"AND GOD WILL WIPE AWAY EVERY
TEAR FROM THEIR EYES."
REVELATION 7:17

Moses's sandals shuffled wearily along the rapidly darkening streets of Pi-Ramesses as he prepared to say goodbye to the land of his birth—a land that had never quite been home. He was born the son of Hebrew slaves yet raised as the son of an Egyptian princess.

Never Egyptian enough for Pharaoh's court.

Forever too Egyptian for his own people.

Moses had always been an outsider.

A balmy evening breeze swept his gray hair back from his forehead. He wore it shorter now than when he'd fled from Pharaoh's wrath so many years before. Years of exile in Midian had freed Moses from most of the outer trappings he had acquired in Egypt. It didn't take long to trade his fine linen tunic for the rough wool of a shepherd's kilt. Gradually, a beard softened the lines of his once clean-shaven face. The dirt and grime of the desert quickly replaced costly Egyptian cosmetics. After all, the sheep and goats didn't care whether his eyes were lined with kohl.

As Moses passed by a home on the right side of the narrow street, an Israelite man ducked beneath the doorway and stood on his threshold. He held a clay pot in one hand and a brush fashioned from hyssop in the other. He carefully dipped the brush into the pot, soaking the hyssop in lamb's blood. Then he solemnly painted the sides and top of the doorframe with blood, a sign of redemption to the destroying angel that would sweep through Egypt in search of the firstborn of every household.

"When I see the blood, I will pass over you," the Lord said (Exodus 12:13).

The scent of roast lamb filled the night air as each family carefully followed God's instructions for the first Passover meal.

Slaughter a lamb without blemish at twilight...
Roast it over the fire...
Not one of its bones is to be broken...

Moses gripped the staff in his right hand a bit tighter. The simple shepherd's staff had become his constant companion as he led his father-in-law's sheep in the hills of Midian. When Moses was sent back to Egypt, God turned it into an instrument of wonder—a sign to all of Egypt that He alone was God.

By God's power the staff became a snake in Moses's hand on command. One dip of the staff into the Nile and the river turned to blood. He waved it over the waters of Egypt, and frogs covered the land. Dust turned to gnats. Thunder, hail, and lightning crashed to the earth. Locusts devoured the land down to the last blade of grass. Boils erupted on the people's skin, darkness blotted out the sun, flies swarmed, and livestock perished. God released plague after plague on Egypt, and still Pharaoh refused to free the children of Abraham from their slavery.

But that was about to change. At midnight, the last plague would fall, and with it, Pharaoh's will. After that, Moses's staff would lead, protect, and guide once again, but this time, instead of sheep, he would tenderly lead God's people out of slavery and into the land of promise.

The night grew darker, colder, and quieter as if the very land was holding its breath. Moses sank down to rest at the city gate and glanced up at the rising moon. It was almost midnight.

A moment later, a long, low wail rose in the distance, shattering the stillness. It was joined by another, and another, until a chorus of grief and loss filled the night. Moses bowed his head in sorrow and turned to face the darkness outside the city walls.

And he waited.

Moses watched as the light of half a dozen reed torches bobbed ever nearer as Pharaoh's officials approached the walls of Pi-Ramesses. Within the hour, he and Aaron were standing before Pharaoh for the final time.

Tall columns, the tops of which were carved into the petals of a lotus flower and gracefully touched the ceiling, lined the space. Detailed reliefs depicting the Pharaoh's military victories, as well as his divinity, covered the walls in brilliant color, awash in the golden glow of lamplight. Pharaoh was seated on his throne as his officials and servants lined the walls, their eyes fixed in terror on the two Hebrews in their midst. An uneasy silence filled the room as Pharaoh struggled to control his emotions. When he spoke at last, his voice trembled.

"Get out of here and be done with you—you and your Israelites!" Pharaoh said. "Go worship GOD on your own terms. And yes, take your sheep and cattle as you've insisted, but go. And bless me" (12:31–32 THE MESSAGE).

When Moses and Aaron walked back through the gate of Pi-Ramesses, they found the city in chaos. Each Israelite home was surrounded by terrified Egyptian neighbors begging them to leave their land. As the Israelites gathered their families, livestock, and their few meager possessions, they fell into line behind Moses. The Egyptians pressed treasures of gold and silver in their hands to speed them on their way.

Once out of the city, Moses turned to look back at the long line of newly freed slaves. Seventy-two of Abraham's descendants entered Egypt in the time of Joseph. Thousands upon thousands now set their eyes and hopes on Canaan. Their faces were gaunt, their eyes fearful, their bodies and hearts broken by the yoke of slavery.

And yet they carried within them God's hope for the world. One day, from that ragged rabble of slaves who had just celebrated their first Passover, would come the Messiah, the Second Adam, born to reverse the curse.

Immanuel,

In the darkest of nights, we wait for the Star of Bethlehem to guide our way.

We wait as captives longing for freedom. We, the wounded and broken, wait for Your healing touch. Ravaged and battered by a world addicted to war, we wait for the Prince of Peace.

Come, perfect Lamb of God who takes away the sins of the world.

We wait for You.

Amen

Star and Scepter

MOSES

BALAAM

JOSHUA

IN THOSE DAYS JOHN THE BAPTIST CAME,
PREACHING IN THE WILDERNESS
OF JUDEA AND SAYING,
"REPENT, FOR THE KINGDOM OF
HEAVEN HAS COME NEAR."
THIS IS HE WHO WAS SPOKEN OF
THROUGH THE PROPHET ISAIAH:
"A VOICE OF ONE CALLING IN THE WILDERNESS,
'PREPARE THE WAY FOR THE LORD,
MAKE STRAIGHT PATHS FOR HIM.'"
MATTHEW 3:1–3

AND HE [ZECHARIAH'S SON] WILL
GO ON BEFORE THE LORD,
IN THE SPIRIT AND POWER OF ELIJAH,
TO TURN THE HEARTS OF THE
PARENTS TO THEIR CHILDREN
AND THE DISOBEDIENT TO THE
WISDOM OF THE RIGHTEOUS—
TO MAKE READY A PEOPLE PREPARED
FOR THE LORD.
LUKE 1:17

Balaam the sorcerer stood on the rock-strewn peak of Mount Pisgah and looked out over the Jordan valley stretched out as far as he could see. Overhead, dark gray clouds were rolling in, casting deep shadows on the hills beneath him. The valley swept along either side of the Jordan River. And there, far beneath him, lay the Israelite encampment.

Tiny figures milled about the camp, tending animals, lighting cooking fires, and visiting with their neighbors. The journey to Canaan should have taken the Israelites no more than a few months, and yet it had lasted for more than forty years—years in which Abraham's descendants learned important lessons of obedience and trust.

Day after day, they pulled up their tent stakes to traverse the same harsh landscape in search of pasture for their flocks until they knew every tree, every stream, each and every stone. Babies were born, young men grew old, old men were buried in the sand, but God had never failed to provide. Manna fell from heaven; water flowed from the rocks; even their cloaks and sandals resisted the ravages of time.

The children of Israel left Egypt as a mass of terrified slaves, but in the wilderness they became a great nation. Laws were established, leadership confirmed, and lessons learned. Now they were ready to take the last steps into the Promised Land. And so, they tended their fires, told stories to their children of God's greatness, and dreamed of home, blissfully unaware that far above them Balak, king of Moab, was gathered with his officials to make sure Israel would go no farther.

Balak, his men, and the great sorcerer Balaam surveyed the vast ocean of tents teeming with men, women, and children. Balak was certain that they would sweep past Moab's borders, consuming everything in their path. He had to stop them before it was too late. Gravely, he turned his attention to Balaam. He was depending on Balaam's curses to cripple the multitude before it surged into Moab.

Balak's eyes never left the sorcerer as Balaam gazed at the swath of tents below. The wind whipped Balaam's long gray hair and beard about his head and tugged at his robe. Slowly he raised his arms and began to sway softly back and forth. His head jerked back, his mouth fell open, and his dark eyes rolled until only the whites remained.

Balak's eyes shone in expectation. He had seen Balaam at work before. The curse on Israel, twice delayed, was imminent.

But then Balaam sighed, his face relaxed, and his shoulders slumped. A moment later, he lifted his eyes to the Israelite camp. When he spoke, his voice was heavy with resignation.

"How beautiful are your tents, Jacob, your dwelling places, Israel," he said. "Like valleys they spread out, like gardens beside a river, like aloes planted by the LORD, like cedars beside the waters. May those who bless you be blessed and those who curse you be cursed!" (Numbers 24:5–6, 9).

"Ugghhhh!" Balak screamed in fury, clenching his fists. "I called you to curse my enemies, but three times now you have blessed them instead. Now get on home! I promised to reward you, but the LORD has kept you from getting the reward" (24:10–11 GNT).

Balaam turned to Balak in exasperation. His reputation as a powerful sorcerer, not to mention an abundance of silver and gold, was slipping through his fingers. He was in no mood for Balak's indignation.

"Did I not tell the messengers you sent me, 'Even if Balak gave me all the silver and gold in his palace, I could not do anything of my own accord, good or bad, to go beyond the command of the LORD—and I must say only what the LORD says'?" (24:12–13).

Balaam turned back to the valley and his eyes settled on the thin blue line of the Jordan River. Slowly, the tents faded away and another scene took their place as God lifted the veil of time.

A crowd was gathered around the river. There, waist-deep in the water, stood a man wearing a prophet's tunic of rough camel hair. Beside him stood another man, a man unlike any other, the Great King who would sit on the throne forever, the bright Morning Star who would break the curse. The prophet baptized the Great King, and when He rose from the water, the heavens opened and the Spirit of God, like a dove, descended upon Him.

When Balaam spoke again, his voice was soft.

> *I see Him, but not now;*
> *I behold Him, but not near.*
> *A star will come out of Jacob;*
> *a scepter will rise out of Israel*
> *(24:17).*

Balak and his officials listened to the prophecy and then turned in defeat to go on their way. Balaam, the once great sorcerer, took one last look at the tents below and felt a shadow of doom in the depths of his soul. Then he turned his back on Israel, and with heavy steps, began the long journey home.

Ancient of Days,

If You are for Your people, who can be against them? You hold fast to Your promises through our most crippling weakness and devastating failures, using even the most unworthy of servants to accomplish Your purposes. You are forever patient, faithful, mighty to save.

Amen

Home
at Last

WHEN ISRAEL CAME OUT OF EGYPT,
JACOB FROM A PEOPLE OF FOREIGN TONGUE,
JUDAH BECAME GOD'S SANCTUARY,
ISRAEL HIS DOMINION.
THE SEA LOOKED AND FLED,
THE JORDAN TURNED BACK;
THE MOUNTAINS LEAPED LIKE RAMS,
THE HILLS LIKE LAMBS.
WHY WAS IT, SEA, THAT YOU FLED?
WHY, JORDAN, DID YOU TURN BACK?
WHY, MOUNTAINS, DID YOU LEAP LIKE RAMS,
YOU HILLS, LIKE LAMBS?
TREMBLE, EARTH, AT THE PRESENCE OF THE LORD,
AT THE PRESENCE OF THE GOD OF JACOB,
WHO TURNED THE ROCK INTO A POOL,
THE HARD ROCK INTO SPRINGS OF WATER.

PSALM 114

Joshua sat on a hillside just outside of the Israelite camp and gazed across the Jordan River in the direction of Jericho. The city was several miles away, but it wasn't difficult for Joshua to imagine the fortifications that awaited Israel. He had seen many cities like Jordan years before, when Moses sent him and eleven other Israelite men on a reconnaissance mission into the land.

The city, built on a tall mound, was secured by two walls. The exterior wall, interspersed by guard towers, bordered the base of the mound. Ringing the city just inside this wall were the homes and shops most vulnerable to attack, and therefore bargain real estate. A bit farther up the mound, a second wall provided added security for the wealthier, more respectable citizens of Jericho. The only entrance to the city was through a massive, six-chambered gate.

Jericho was located in a vibrant oasis and positioned to control one of the most important crossings of the Jordan River. The inhabitants were well-armed and trained, accustomed to defending their city for centuries from those who longed to take their abundant provision and powerful position as their own. As Israel moved forward to possess the Promised Land, they could not afford to leave mighty Jericho at their backs. They had to take the city. As Moses's successor, Joshua knew that leading them into that formidable battle was up to him.

Joshua leaned back onto the grassy hillside, closed his eyes, and turned his heavily tanned, lined face up to the warmth of the spring sun. There, in the stillness of his soul, God spoke.

"Moses My servant is dead. Now then, you and all these people, get ready to cross the Jordan River into the land I am about to give to them—to the Israelites. I will give you every place where you set your foot, as I promised Moses. Your territory will extend from the desert to Lebanon, and from the great river, the Euphrates—all the Hittite country—to the Mediterranean Sea in the west" (Joshua 1:2–4).

Joshua sat up and once again looked toward the Promised Land. God promised the land was flowing with milk and honey, a truth Joshua had seen with his own eyes, but he also knew there were fierce battles and daunting challenges ahead. Would Israel, this people who had so often proved themselves desperately vulnerable to temptation, mutiny, and a forgetfulness of God's goodness, rise to the occasion?

"No one will be able to stand against you all the days of your life," God reassured Joshua. *"As I was with Moses, so I will be with you; I will never leave you nor forsake you. Be strong and courageous, because you will lead these people to inherit the land I swore to their ancestors to give them"* (1:5–6).

I will be with you...
I will never leave or forsake you...
Be strong and courageous...

God's promises fell one after the other upon Joshua's anxious heart, blanketing every insecurity and whispering solace to every fear. Joshua would lead Israel, but he would not lead Israel alone. God would go with him, walk beside him, show him the way. God would remain faithful to His promises to Abraham. Israel would inherit the land.

Three days later, Joshua stood at the banks of the swollen Jordan River as the first rays of sunlight crept over the surface of the deep, fast-moving, muddy water. Relentless rains upstream had pushed the Jordan past its banks, transforming the river into a monster.

This morning, Joshua was not alone. All of Israel was amassed behind him, tying the last of their possessions to the backs of donkeys and corralling livestock. Mothers strapped their babies to their backs as fathers scooped up toddlers to ride on their shoulders, each of them fearfully eyeing the raging river between them and God's promise.

Joshua understood their trepidation. Only a few of them were old enough to have learned to swim in Egypt. The rest had never been in water that was more than calf-deep. Even if they all had known how to swim, the rapid-flowing, turbulent floodwaters of the Jordan River were deadly.

Joshua looked down at his own aging feet, strapped in the same sandals in which he had walked out of Egypt forty years before. Even after countless miles over sand and stone, the soles were sturdy. Not even a strap was frayed. He picked up the edge of his linen robe. It was soft and smooth, exactly the same condition as it had been the night God parted the Red Sea. Then Joshua lifted his eyes to the Jordan River.

God would provide.

Joshua turned to the priests, and the ark of the covenant between them. The rectangular box of acacia wood was overlaid with pure gold. Two poles, also overlaid with gold, ran through two golden rings on each side of the ark. The lid bore the sculptures of two cherubim, one on each end, bowed toward each other, their wings touching.

"Take up the ark of the covenant and pass on ahead of the people," Joshua said (3:6).

The four priests each grasped one end of the poles, lifted the ark into the air, and solemnly made their way to the edge of the Jordan. The crowd grew silent, their eyes fixed on the golden ark, the representation of God's presence among them.

Carefully, the first two priests stepped onto the rocky bottom of the Jordan as the rushing water tugged at the hem of their robes. They took a few cautious steps forward to make room for the two priests at the back of the ark to join them.

As the last priest's foot dipped beneath the water, a distant rumbling reached the Israelites from upstream. A moment later, the water from upstream narrowed to a trickle and then stopped completely.

As the priests stood in the midst of the Jordan, Joshua led the people to the other side. For a moment he stood at the riverbank watching as men, women, and children stepped out of the river bed and into the land of promise.

Abraham's children were home at last.

That night they set up camp at Gilgal, and on the fourteenth day of the month they celebrated Passover in the Promised Land for the first time. The next day, the nutty scent of roasting grain filled the camp as Israel ate of the produce of Canaan. Throughout the camp there were cries of joy as they tasted grain for the first time since leaving Egypt.

That night, Israel drifted off to sleep with full stomachs and hopeful hearts, but Joshua knew their most harrowing danger had never been in whether or not there was food in the pot, or shelter over their heads. God was faithful to provide.

The most perilous challenge Israel faced had always been the same: Would they remember God...or would they forget Him?

"When the LORD your God brings you into the land He swore to your fathers, to Abraham, Isaac and Jacob, to give you—a land with large, flourishing cities you did not build, houses filled with all kinds of good things you did not provide, wells you did not dig, and vineyards and olive groves you did not plant—then when you eat and are satisfied, be careful that you do not forget the LORD, who brought you out of Egypt, out of the land of slavery" (Deuteronomy 6:10–12).

Father,

When I think of Israel's forgetfulness of You, my heart is broken because I know I am guilty of forgetting You too. How strange that this time of year when I should most readily focus on the gift of Your Son, I find myself so easily distracted by the trappings of the season. Remind me, Father, that You speak in the quiet. Help me make space for You this Advent.

Amen

Wheat in a Winepress

AFTER JOSHUA'S DEATH, A GENERATION WAS BORN
WHO FORGOT GOD AND ALL HE HAD DONE FOR ISRAEL. AND
SO, ISRAEL DID AN EVIL THING; SHE ABANDONED HER GOD
AND WORSHIPED BAAL. SHE FORGOT THE GOD WHO DELIVERED
HER FROM EGYPT AND BEGAN TO WORSHIP THE GODS OF THE
CANAANITES, BAAL AND ASHTORETH. AND GOD WAS JEALOUS
FOR HIS PEOPLE, DEEPLY CONCERNED FOR THEM, FOR THEY
HAD LOST THEIR WAY. SO, GOD REMOVED HIS HAND OF PROTEC-
TION AND FAVOR FROM THEM, AND THE RAIDERS FROM MIDIAN
RUSHED IN, DESCENDING LIKE LOCUSTS, DESTROYING EVERY-
THING IN THEIR PATH. BUT THEN GOD, IN HIS MERCY, RAISED
UP JUDGES TO DELIVER HIS PEOPLE.
JUDGES 2:10–16 (PARAPHRASED)

AFTER THAT WHOLE GENERATION HAD BEEN GATHERED TO
THEIR ANCESTORS, ANOTHER GENERATION GREW UP WHO KNEW
NEITHER THE LORD NOR WHAT HE HAD DONE FOR ISRAEL. THEN
THE ISRAELITES DID EVIL IN THE EYES OF THE LORD AND
SERVED THE BAALS. THEY FORSOOK THE LORD, THE GOD
OF THEIR ANCESTORS, WHO HAD BROUGHT THEM OUT OF
EGYPT. THEY FOLLOWED AND WORSHIPED VARIOUS GODS OF
THE PEOPLES AROUND THEM. THEY AROUSED THE LORD'S
ANGER BECAUSE THEY FORSOOK HIM AND SERVED BAAL
AND THE ASHTORETHS. IN HIS ANGER AGAINST ISRAEL
THE LORD GAVE THEM INTO THE HANDS OF RAIDERS WHO
PLUNDERED THEM. HE SOLD THEM INTO THE HANDS OF THEIR
ENEMIES ALL AROUND, WHOM THEY WERE NO LONGER ABLE TO
RESIST. WHENEVER ISRAEL WENT OUT TO FIGHT, THE HAND OF
THE LORD WAS AGAINST THEM TO DEFEAT THEM, JUST AS HE
HAD SWORN TO THEM. THEY WERE IN GREAT DISTRESS. THEN
THE LORD RAISED UP JUDGES, WHO SAVED THEM OUT OF THE
HANDS OF THESE RAIDERS.
JUDGES 2:10–16

AND GOD COULD BEAR ISRAEL'S MISERY NO MORE.
JUDGES 10:16 (PARAPHRASED)

Gideon tossed the final sheaf of wheat onto the floor of the winepress and then sighed in discouragement at the sight of the meager pile of grain at his feet. He took the heavy stick he had used as a staff on the way up the terraced hillside and threw it on top of the pile. Then he walked to the rock wall that overlooked the centuries-old terraces below and the valley beyond.

The terraces should have been verdant with late-spring growth on the vines. Instead, they were barren, littered with uprooted plants, jumbles of broken vines, and withered leaves. Gideon closed his eyes and envisioned the hillside in its better days, long before Israel had turned away from God. The Lord had tired of Israel's idolatry of the Canaanite fertility god, Baal, and the injustice and violence that flowed in its wake. He withdrew His protection from Israel and allowed the Midianites to flood into the land like a swarm of locust, destroying every crop in their path.

In the days before the invasion, the winepress was a place of joyful celebration. Gideon could still see the dark-purple grapes spread across the plastered floor of the press. He could hear the happy laughter of his family and friends as the men trod the grapes barefoot, keeping rhythm with the musicians who played in the shade of the ancient oak just outside the winepress wall. The winepress was a place of community and celebration. It was a place of joy.

And now, it lay barren and desolate except for the meager harvest of wheat that Gideon had brought to the winepress, instead of the threshing floor, in an attempt to hide it from the Midianites.

It would be a long time before songs of joy were played at the winepress once again. It took years of careful cultivation before a grapevine yielded a harvest. Now, the best the winepress could offer them was a bit of bread for tomorrow.

The spring sun was warm on Gideon's back as he walked back across the winepress floor and bent to pick up the stick that lay on top of the wheat. Then he crouched down in front of the pile and began to beat it, forcing the tough chaff to break apart and fall away from the grain. He flailed the grain until the muscles in his back, arms, and shoulders burned and sweat rolled down his forehead and cheeks, soaking his beard. At last, panting for breath, he stood up and dropped the stick to the ground. He grasped the edge of the wall and twisted to his right in an effort to release the knots in the muscles of his back. After a moment, he switched his hand position and twisted to the left. When he did, he let out a cry of surprise to find a man sitting against the trunk of the oak tree, a staff resting across his lap.

The man beneath the oak was looking out across the valley, past trampled crops and abandoned homes. His eyes strayed to the hillside across the valley where Israelite families had taken shelter in caves to hide from the Midianite raiders. "The LORD is with you, mighty warrior," the man said softly (Judges 6:12).

Gideon laughed bitterly, wiped the sweat from his eyes, and rested his hands on his hips, gasping for breath. "Pardon me, my lord," Gideon replied, "but if the LORD is with us, why has all this happened to us? Where are all His wonders that our ancestors told us about when they said, 'Did not the LORD bring us up out of Egypt?' But now the LORD has abandoned us and given us into the hand of Midian" (6:13).

The man turned to look at Gideon. "Go in the strength you have and save Israel out of Midian's hand. Am I not sending you?" (6:14).

The color drained from Gideon's face, and he took a step backward. Something in the man's eyes spoke of authority and power. Perhaps, he thought with a shudder, this was not a man at all…

"Pardon me, my lord," Gideon replied, his voice trembling, "but how can *I* save Israel? My clan is the weakest in Manasseh, and I am the least in my family" (6:15 emphasis added).

"I will be with you," the man said, "and you will strike down all the Midianites, leaving none alive" (6:16).

Gideon attempted to swallow but found his mouth as dry as the sand. He dropped his eyes to the ground and clasped his hands together in an effort to still their shaking.

"If now I have found favor in your eyes, give me a sign that it is really You talking to me," Gideon replied. "Please do not go away until I come back and bring my offering and set it before You" (6:17–18).

"I will wait until you return," the man said, and then turned once again to look out over the valley below (6:18).

Gideon hurried home, where he prepared a young goat and unleavened bread. He placed the meat and bread in a basket and poured the broth from the lamb in a pot. When he arrived back at the winepress with his offerings in hand, he was relieved to find the man still sitting peacefully beneath the oak.

When Gideon drew near, the man picked up his staff and pointed to a nearby rock. "Take the meat and the unleavened bread, place them on this rock, and pour out the broth" (6:20).

Gideon carefully removed the meat and bread from the basket and arranged them on the rock. Then he poured the broth over them. When he had completed his task, he stepped back and turned to the man beside him. The man beneath the oak bent forward, stretching His staff toward the rock and the offering it held. Then He touched the tip of His staff to the meat.

The rock beneath the offering immediately began glowing as if it had been thrown into the fire, growing brighter and brighter. Gideon raised his hand to his face to block the waves of blistering heat radiating off of it. The meat sizzled and popped, and then a roaring fire roared out of the rock, consuming every last crumb of the sacrifice. Then the blaze abruptly vanished.

When Gideon turned to face the man beneath the tree, He was gone.

Gideon fell to the ground, covering his face with his hands in terror. "Alas, Sovereign LORD! I have seen the angel of the LORD face to face!" he cried (6:22).

"Peace!" the Lord said to him. "Do not be afraid. You are not going to die" (6:23).

Slowly, Gideon lowered his trembling hands from his face and reached down to the ground. He picked up a rock, then another and another, stacking one on top of the other until an altar stood upon the charred stone where the Lord had consumed Gideon's offering with fire.

When the last rock was laid, Gideon placed his hand on top of the altar, closed his eyes, and whispered the altar's name:

Jehovah-Shalom...

The Lord is peace.

That night, while the village lay sleeping, Gideon and ten of his servants stood in the moonlight before his father's altar to Baal, who was believed to control the dew and rain necessary for a successful harvest. Gideon walked up to the altar and grasped the bronze statue of a bull, no larger than a newborn goat. He held it in his hands for a moment and thought of all the sacrifices offered to it, the brutal depths of betrayal Israel had inflicted upon her Creator through her worship of a god fashioned by the hands of men, all in the hope that they could manipulate their false god into sending dew and rain when Israel needed it most.

But there was only one true God. He alone parted the Red Sea and delivered His people. He alone fed them with manna in the wilderness. He alone fulfilled every promise He made to their father, Abraham.

He alone sent the dew and the rain.

Gideon threw the idol to the ground in disgust. Then nine of his servants proceeded to destroy the altar, as well as a nearby Asherah pole, before building an altar to the God of their fathers, the God of Abraham, Isaac, and Jacob, the God who was ever faithful to provide.

One servant stood to the side, watching the others. In his hand was the tether to the animal God had instructed Gideon to bring as an offering.

A bull, seven years old.

When morning dawned, all that remained of the bull was ashes. The embers of the fire on the altar grew cold. Gideon surveyed the hillside, now redeemed. It was the first of many battles he would fight to return Israel's heart to her God.

Her Maker. Her Deliverer. Her Provider.

The God of the dew and the rain.

My Provider,

How forgetful I am of You. Forgetful of Your goodness. Forgetful of Your mercies. Forgetful of all the ways You have shown Yourself faithful to me.

I grow so attached to the provision in my hand. Like a petulant child, I cling to it. But You, my gracious God, call me to let it go so that You might bring fresh provision, deeper faith, a new and beautiful calling...

Forgive me, Abba. Make my heart true. In this season in which the world screams for more, and more and more, grant me the courage to abandon all to You.

Amen

House of Bread

GIDEON

NAOMI

SAMUEL

Bethlehem: House of Bread

"BUT YOU, BETHLEHEM EPHRATHAH,

THOUGH YOU ARE SMALL AMONG

THE CLANS OF JUDAH,

OUT OF YOU WILL COME FOR ME

ONE WHO WILL BE RULER OVER ISRAEL,

WHOSE ORIGINS ARE FROM OF OLD,

FROM ANCIENT TIMES."

THEREFORE ISRAEL WILL BE ABANDONED

UNTIL THE TIME WHEN SHE WHO

IS IN LABOR BEARS A SON,

AND THE REST OF HIS BROTHERS RETURN

TO JOIN THE ISRAELITES.

HE WILL STAND AND SHEPHERD HIS FLOCK

IN THE STRENGTH OF THE LORD,

IN THE MAJESTY OF THE NAME

OF THE LORD HIS GOD.

AND THEY WILL LIVE SECURELY,

FOR THEN HIS GREATNESS

WILL REACH TO THE ENDS OF THE EARTH.

MICAH 5:2–4

The house was quiet. So very quiet.

The last of the mourners were gone, the burials complete. The most violent waves of her grief had receded from shore, leaving barrenness and desolation behind.

That morning, the morning after her sons were laid in their tombs, Naomi had prepared a simple meal for her and her young daughters-in law. Orpah fetched the water from the town well. Ruth swept the floors clean.

Now the three of them sat silently, each lost in her own sorrow. Naomi looked down at her hands where they rested in her lap. For so much of her life, it seemed her hands never stilled as she cared for her husband and two sons. Wasn't it only yesterday that she held her chubby baby boys in her lap as they smiled and cooed? Was it just a dream that she once held them close, counting their fingers and kissing their tiny toes?

Her hands were so...idle. There was nothing left to do, no one left to care for. All was still. All was quiet. When Naomi left her home in Bethlehem ten years before, her life was full. Now, there was only empty.

It was time to go home.

Slowly, she rose from her chair and began to pack her few belongings—an extra tunic, some bread for the journey, the small pouch of silver hidden behind a brick in the wall. Before the sun was high in the sky, Naomi was ready to go. She slung her bag across her back and left home, her daughters-in law following anxiously behind her.

When Naomi reached the road that led home to Judah, she sighed, put down her bag, turned to them, and took each of them by the hand.

"Go back, each of you, to your mother's home. May the LORD show you kindness, as you have shown kindness to your dead husbands and to me. May the LORD grant that each of you will find rest in the home of another husband," Naomi said (Ruth 1:8–9).

The girls began weeping, and begging her to allow them to come with her. Eventually, Naomi convinced Orpah to return to her family, but Ruth could not be persuaded. "Where you go I will go, and where you stay I will stay," Ruth insisted. "Your people will be my people and your God my God" (1:16).

And so the two widows—one a wandering daughter headed home, the other leaving all she knew to become a stranger in a foreign land—began the journey to the land of God's promise.

They walked down from the lush mountaintop plateau of Moab, down, down the steep mountainside as the morning grew hot. Then they faced the Dead Sea stretched out before them. Its banks were strewn with eerie salt pillars and blanketed with salt flats that glistened in the sun. The glare shone its rays with such brutal force that Naomi and Ruth bowed their heads low to shield their eyes from its brilliance. They paced across the natural land bridge with slow, deliberate steps, and then along the shore until the road led across the sweeping, barren wilderness. And then, the topography flattened. Mountains and sand gave way to fields of golden barley ripe for harvest, gently rustling in the breeze. Men and women dotted the fields, cutting the grain and piling it high, preparing it for the threshing floors. They had reached Bethlehem, Israel's "House of Bread." Naomi was home.

As Naomi and Ruth passed, the reapers paused in their work to curiously watch the two strangers go by. Then suddenly one woman's eyes grew wide with recognition. "Can this be Naomi?" she asked her companions.

Naomi paused, closed her eyes for a moment, and then turned to the women in the fields. Women she had played with as children, gossiped with as girls. Women who had celebrated with her when she married Elimelech. Women who had held her babies, then watched them grow into boys, tall and strong.

"Don't call me Naomi," she told them. "Call me Mara, because the Almighty has made my life very bitter. I went away full, but the LORD has brought me back empty. Why call me Naomi? The LORD has afflicted me; the Almighty has brought misfortune upon me" (1:20–21).

Ruth waited patiently as Naomi stood for a moment with her hand resting on the wooden front door of the flat-roofed, stone home she had once shared with Elimelech and her sons. After a moment, Naomi took a deep breath and shoved open the door. A waft of stale air met the two women as they stepped into the dim interior. Before them, stairs led up into the main living area. Another set of stairs to their left descended into the basement stable.

With heavy steps Naomi led the way upstairs. She unshouldered her bag and dropped it heavily to the floor. Sunlight fell from four small windows near the roofline and through gaps in the deteriorating thatched roof. Illuminated dust motes floated in the air. Naomi walked along the back wall of the room and through the doorway at the corner to gaze into the *kataluma*, the guest room, beyond it. A few jars heavily coated in dust sat in the corner. Otherwise, the room was empty, just as the family had left it.

Niches pocketed three walls of the room awaiting sleeping mats, clothing, and other necessities, but the front of the room was open to the stable below. The floor of the main room sloped gently toward the stable, where two oval mangers were carved into the floor near the edge, an arrangement that allowed hungry animals to simply peek over the edge for a bit of hay.

Naomi walked back into the main living area and past the cold plastered mud-brick oven to pick up a stack of bowls resting on a long wooden shelf. She blew the dust off of them, set them back, then brushed her hands together to clean them off. Then she tugged at the cord around her neck to pull her money pouch from beneath her robe. She untied it, plucked a couple of coins from it, and placed them in Ruth's palm.

"Go to the market," she told her daughter-in-law. "Buy a bit of grain and some oil for the lamp. I will gather some sticks to get a fire started and clean up a bit."

As Ruth turned to leave the room, she cast one last glance back over her shoulder to find Naomi with broom in hand, sweeping ten years of dust and broken dreams into the stable below.

Days slipped past and, bit by bit, Naomi and Ruth reclaimed their home from years of neglect. Surfaces were dusted, the floors swept clean. At night a fire in the oven joined the oil lamp on its stone shelf in driving the shadows from the corners. But each day, the money pouch grew lighter until the morning when Naomi and Ruth sat down to their last meal of grain.

They ate slowly, silently. When the last grain of roasted barley was gone, Ruth reached over and placed her hand on Naomi's arm.

"Let me go to the fields to gather the grain that the harvest workers leave," she said. "I am sure to find someone who will let me work with him" (2:2 GNT).

Naomi looked into her beloved daughter-in-law's eyes. So young. So vulnerable. It would be dangerous enough for any girl her age to go out into the fields unprotected, but especially so for a foreigner. Then Naomi looked back into their empty bowls before lifting a hand to her chest, where the empty money pouch rested beneath her robe.

What choice did they have?

"Go ahead, my daughter," she said.

Ruth nodded, reached over to hug Naomi good-bye, and then hurried out the door, leaving Naomi to watch the shadows creep across the wall.

And pray.

As the sun dipped low on the horizon, Naomi began pacing back and forth across the room. Every few minutes she stopped to listen, sure she heard the sound of footsteps in the courtyard, only to find it was simply the sounds of another day in Bethlehem drawing to a close. Men were greeting their families as they came in from the fields. Women were bringing in the wash or scolding the children playing in the street. Naomi sighed in frustration and returned to her pacing. Finally, in exhaustion, she slumped down onto the bench that ran along the wall, buried her face in her hands, and tried to slow her racing heart.

Naomi cried out with a start as the front door banged open and Ruth noisily made her way up the stairs. Naomi stared wide-eyed at the girl when she rounded the corner beaming with joy and struggling to carry a large sack of grain.

"Where did you glean today?" Naomi asked Ruth in astonishment. "Where did you work? Blessed be the man who took notice of you!" (2:19).

Ruth told Naomi about a kind man named Boaz, who had not only welcomed her to glean in his fields but treated her with the same kindness and protection with which he cared for his own servant girls. He even went so far as to instruct the reapers to deliberately drop extra grain for her as they worked.

And something dawned within Naomi. Deep in her spirit that had so long been dark with loss and grief flickered a ray of hope. God, perhaps, was still kind. Just maybe He had not forgotten her after all.

"The LORD bless him!" Naomi said to her daughter-in-law. "He has not stopped showing His kindness to the living and the dead." She added, "That man is our close relative; he is one of our guardian-redeemers" (2:20).

Ruth continued to glean in the fields of Boaz throughout the harvest. And in an Israel that had pervasively forgotten her God and turned to the worship of idols and allowed violence and brutal exploitation of the vulnerable, Boaz steadfastly remained the exception. He carefully followed God's law, treated his servants with justice and decency, and tenderly protected the vulnerable.

On the last night of the harvest, Boaz and his men spent the night on the threshing floor tossing grain into the air so that the evening breezes could carry the chaff away. And Naomi took a leap of faith.

"Come, my daughter," she said to Ruth. "Boaz is our close relative, one of our kinsmen-redeemers who, according to God's law, bears the responsibility of marrying my son's widow to provide for her and preserve the family inheritance. Get ready! Go to him tonight when he is winnowing barley on the threshing floor, and when he lays down to sleep, uncover his feet and lie down. When he realizes you are there, ask him if he will be your kinsman-redeemer."

Boaz joyfully received God's commandment to fulfill his responsibility as a kinsmen-redeemer. Ruth, a widow and a foreigner, became the wife of a wealthy, respected man. Naomi, broken and empty, became the matriarch of their family once again. Memories of scarcity were swept away by the sweetness of abundance.

But God was not finished.

Ruth conceived and bore a son. They took the child and placed him in Naomi's arms. She laid him on her lap, counted his tiny fingers, and kissed his little toes.

"Naomi has a son!" the women of the village exclaimed in wonder (4:17).

They named the child Obed. He became the father of Jesse, who was the father of David, the second king of Israel.

Redeemer,

I hold before You all the places in my life that are empty, the desolate wastelands of betrayal, loss, and grief. I lift to You my most bitter failures and my most precious, shattered hopes.

You are the God of the barren, the mender of the broken. You forever remain my sure, impossible hope. This Advent, this holy season of expectation, I wait for You.

Come, Emmanuel. Come...

Amen

Israel Demands a King

SAMUEL

THE LORD REIGNS FOREVER;
HE HAS ESTABLISHED HIS THRONE FOR JUDGMENT.
HE RULES THE WORLD IN RIGHTEOUSNESS
AND JUDGES THE PEOPLES WITH EQUITY.
THE LORD IS A REFUGE FOR THE OPPRESSED,
A STRONGHOLD IN TIMES OF TROUBLE.
THOSE WHO KNOW YOUR NAME TRUST IN YOU,
FOR YOU, LORD, HAVE NEVER
FORSAKEN THOSE WHO SEEK YOU.

PSALM 9:7–10

S amuel!"

The voice of God called to Samuel as the old man lay dreaming of his boyhood...

He was in the tabernacle at Shiloh, resting on the floor between the lamp and the ark of the covenant. The lamp of God was burning low, its wavering light creeping across the floor and casting strange shadows on the walls. The night was filled with a holy stillness.

"Samuel!"

The child sat up and pushed his long dark hair out of his eyes before turning to face the ark. "Speak," he said, "...Your servant is listening" (I Samuel 3:10).

Samuel awoke and gasped as he sat up in bed and his dream of when God first called to him faded away. The aged man of God rubbed his eyes and then buried his face in his hands. His long, gray hair tumbled over his shoulders down onto the bed, revealing a lifetime of tresses never shorn. For Samuel was a Nazirite.

His mother had dedicated his life to God while he was still in the womb. No wine had ever touched his lips. No razor had touched his head. Never once had he touched the dead, not even when his own precious mother was buried.

Samuel was only five years old when his mother led him by the hand to Shiloh to serve from that time forward in the house of the Lord. And he had done so faithfully. Judge after judge had served Israel since the time of Joshua, each of them called by God to deliver Israel from her oppressors and turn her idolatrous heart back to Him. Some, like Samson, were deeply flawed. Others, like Deborah, were courageous and righteous.

But none had led Israel with the same steadfast devotion to God and country as Samuel. Now, Israel was no longer content to be led by the invisible hand of God, no longer satisfied that she alone out of all the nations in the world heard the word of the Almighty spoken through His prophets and judges. Israel wanted more.

She wanted more tangible evidence of provision and protection.

The elders, somber and determined, had filled Samuel's courtyard and demanded a change.

"Look, you're an old man, and your sons aren't following in your footsteps," the elders said to him. "Here's what we want you to do: Appoint a king to rule us, just like everybody else" (8:5 THE MESSAGE).

Just like everybody else.

Samuel shook his head in disbelief at the memory of their absurd request. For generations, Israel's king was the God of the universe, a King who was forever faithful and forgiving, a King who ruled with justice and wisdom. Instead, Israel wanted a king "like everybody else," a human king like the nations surrounding them. A king who would tax them and oppress them. A king who would serve himself first and at their expense.

What was Samuel to do with this stubborn, ungrateful people?

Samuel had sought God's guidance for Israel countless times since that first night the Lord called his name in the tabernacle. Now, on the darkest of nights, he lifted his hands and face to heaven and waited for God's direction once again.

"Speak, Lord, Your servant is listening," Samuel prayed.

God, as always, was faithful to respond.

"Listen to all that the people are saying to you" the Lord said. *"It is not you they have rejected, but they have rejected Me as their king. As they have done from the day I brought them up out of Egypt until this day, forsaking Me and serving other gods, so they are doing to you. Now listen to them; but warn them solemnly and let them know what the king who will reign over them will claim as his rights"* (8:7–9).

Brokenhearted and sick with loss, Samuel wept.

Slowly, Samuel walked through the streets of Ramah, making his way toward the entrance of the city where God promised to show him the man who would be Israel's first king. When Samuel neared the city gate, he paused, carefully scanning the face of each man entering.

Then he saw him. Handsome. Muscular. So tall he stood head and shoulders over every other man around him. He strode into the city confidently, his head held high.

"This is the man I spoke to you about," the Lord said to Samuel; *"he will govern My people"* (9:17).

The man's name was Saul, and he was from the small but war-like tribe of Benjamin, the only son of a wealthy man.

Israel would love him. He was everything she wanted in a king.

That night, the great hall filled with the most prominent citizens of Ramah. Samuel entered the hall for the feast with the tall and handsome stranger at his side, and the room grew quiet. Purposefully, Samuel led Saul to the head of the table and sat him in the seat of honor. When the meal was served and Samuel honored Saul by serving him the choicest cut of meat, the other guests' eyes grew wide in surprise.

When the feast was over, Samuel took Saul back to his home, where the two men talked late into the night. The prophet did all he could to prepare Israel's new king to lead well. When morning broke, Samuel walked Saul through the quiet streets of sleepy Ramah to send him on his way.

When they neared the gate, Samuel placed a hand on Saul's arm and said, "Wait, I have a word of God for you," as he drew a small flask of oil from his robe.

Samuel reached up to place his hand on the back of Saul's neck and gently motioned for the future king of Israel to bow before him. Samuel lifted the flask and tilted it. A thin stream of green olive oil shimmered in the early-morning sun as it trickled down into Saul's hair. Samuel straightened the flask, sealed it shut, and tucked the vial back in his robe. Then he placed a hand on each of Saul's shoulders and kissed him on the cheek.

"Do you see what this means?" Samuel asked him somberly, searching his face to see if Saul understood the honor and weighty responsibility God was entrusting to him. "GOD has anointed you prince over His people" (10:1 THE MESSAGE).

Saul nodded solemnly as he considered the daunting task before him. Israel faced threats from the Ammonites and Moabites in the east, and the Edomites and Amalekites in the south. These old enemies were joined by a new and terrifying menace invading from Israel's western coast, the Philistines. Internally, tribal jealousies and disunion threatened to tear the country apart.

How could he, Saul, from the tiny tribe of Benjamin, rule Israel?

But God would not leave Saul without aid. A moment later, Saul turned to leave Samuel to return home. As he did, the Spirit of God fell upon him, empowering him with everything he needed to lead Israel well.

If only...Saul obeyed the Lord.

Years later, Samuel sat alone on the floor of his dimly lit home, his back resting against the mud brick wall. Beside him, the ashes in the hearth had long grown cold. The lamp on its niche in the wall remained unlit. Periodically, villagers would stop by, calling to the man of God through the locked door.

Samuel didn't answer. He simply sat near the ashes, utterly still, as tears slipped one after another down his weathered cheeks and into his beard.

The voice of God broke through the silence.

"How long will you mourn for Saul," God asked Samuel, *"since I have rejected him as king over Israel?"* (16:1).

Samuel struggled to stifle a sob. For twenty-five years, he had worked alongside Saul as he served, successfully, as Israel's first king. Then, somehow, God's anointed lost his way. He began to trust too fully in his own prowess, his God-given victories. He began to glorify himself instead of the God who took him from nothing to make him a king.

The last time Samuel saw Saul, it was for the purpose of telling him that God had rejected him as king.

"Does the LORD delight in burnt offerings and sacrifices as much as in obeying the LORD?" Samuel demanded of Saul in frustration. "To obey is better than sacrifice, and to heed is better than the fat of rams" (15:22).

Outward religion failed to reach the heart of not only Saul but Israel as well. It was their fatal flaw. Somehow they missed the truth that God wanted more than rote rituals and empty ceremonies. He wanted their devotion. As Samuel turned to leave Saul that fateful day, Saul grasped the hem of Samuel's robe in panic, leaving a tear.

Tearfully, Samuel turned to Saul and, with finality and regret, pronounced God's judgment. "The LORD has torn the kingdom of Israel from you today and has given it to one of your neighbors—to one better than you. He who is the Glory of Israel does not lie or change His mind; for He is not a man, that He should change His mind" (15:28–29).

Now, tenderly, God broke through Samuel's grief—the time for mourning was over. The moment had come to begin anew. *"Fill your horn with oil and be on your way; I am sending you to Jesse of Bethlehem. I have chosen one of his sons to be king"* (16:1).

When Samuel arrived in Bethlehem, he called Jesse and his sons to stand before him. The eldest son, Eliab, stepped forward. Like Saul, he was handsome and tall, the perfect image of a king.

But he was not God's choice.

"Do not consider his appearance or his height," God said to Samuel, *"for I have rejected him. The LORD does not look at the things people look at. People look at the outward appearance, but the LORD looks at the heart"* (16:7).

One by one, seven sons presented themselves to Samuel, each in turn rejected by God. In dismay, Samuel turned to Jesse. "Are these all the sons you have?" he asked (16:11).

"There is still the youngest," Jesse answered. "He is tending the sheep (16:11)."

"Send for him," Samuel said (16:11).

The older brothers looked at each other skeptically. What could the man of God want with fifteen-year-old David? He was considered so inconsequential, he was assigned the lowliest of all responsibilities: tending the sheep.

A moment later, one of the servants arrived with David in tow. He had auburn hair, just the first hint of a beard, and wore a dirty tunic that smelled like sheep. He held a staff in his hand and had a sling tucked into his belt.

God said to Samuel, *"Rise and anoint him; this is the one"* (16:12).

Samuel stood and began to unseal the horn of oil as he walked toward the boy. Then he anointed the least of Jesse's sons in the presence of his older brothers. Immediately the Spirit of God left Saul and filled David.

A lowly shepherd boy would become Israel's greatest king—a man after God's own heart.

King of all kings,

With Samuel, my heart mourns for Saul. I see in this failed king of Israel my own most harrowing weaknesses: Ingratitude. Pride. A forgetfulness of You.

Forgive me, Father, for the moments I am wooed by praise, distracted by ambition, and enamored with my own success. Pour out Your spirit on me and make me as a humble child after Your own heart.

Amen

A Tale of Two Kings

SAMUEL

DAVID

SOLOMON

HE CHOSE DAVID HIS SERVANT
AND TOOK HIM FROM THE SHEEP PENS;
FROM TENDING THE SHEEP HE BROUGHT HIM
TO BE THE SHEPHERD OF HIS PEOPLE JACOB,
OF ISRAEL HIS INHERITANCE.
AND DAVID SHEPHERDED THEM
WITH INTEGRITY OF HEART;
WITH SKILLFUL HANDS HE LED THEM.
PSALM 78:70—72

Saul sat alone in his tent in the center of his army's encampment nestled in the Valley of Elah. On the other side of the valley lay the camp of the Philistine army.

Every day for a month the battle lines had been drawn, and twice each day Israel's army fled in terror. Goliath, the Philistine champion, roared out of the Philistine line and demanded Israel bring their own champion to fight him in hand-to-hand combat. No one in Saul's army could face him. The situation was dire.

The Valley of Elah was a crucial buffer zone between the coast where the Philistines had invaded and the mountains of Judah. In order for Judah to rest secure, it was essential the Valley of Elah remain under Israel's control. Now, not only was the valley threatened but it was fully occupied by Philistine forces. If Israel failed, the Philistine army would sweep toward Bethlehem, destroying everything in its path.[1]

To no avail, Saul offered generous benefits to any warrior possessing the courage to face Goliath. The powerful Philistine stood nine feet tall, wearing 125 pounds of brass armor. Facing Goliath in combat would have required incredible bravery from an Israelite warrior in the best of times, but after the Spirit of God left Saul, morale was low. The king was no longer a fearless voice of decisive leadership. Day after day he sat alone, deeply depressed, trying but failing to summon the energy to face the Philistine threat. And so, morning and evening day after day, the Philistine giant roared out of the battle line, blaspheming God and demanding that Israel produce a champion.

And each time, bereft of a leader, Israel fled.

After Jesse's youngest son, David, was anointed king of Israel, Samuel returned to Ramah, David returned to his sheep, and his

---

[1] James C. Martin, John A. Beck, and David G. Hansen, *A Visual Guide to Bible Events* (Grand Rapids, MI: Baker, 2009), 84.

older brothers went to war. As the weeks drew on with his sons on the battle lines, Jesse grew anxious. Finally, he sent David to take them supplies and to see that they were safe.

On day forty of the conflict, David arrived in the Israelite encampment as evening fell. The rumble of warriors falling into line and the roar of a battle cry reached his ears from the valley below. Quickly, David left his supplies with a servant and rushed to the battle lines to find his brothers. Just as he found them, Goliath swaggered out into the wide swath of land separating the battle lines.

"Why do you come out and line up for battle?" Goliath bellowed as he prowled back and forth in front of Israel's army. "Am I not a Philistine, and are you not the servants of Saul? Choose a man and have him come down to me. If he is able to fight and kill me, we will become your subjects; but if I overcome him and kill him, you will become our subjects and serve us" (I Samuel 17:8–9).

The Philistine army erupted in raucous laughter and shrill battle cries as Goliath turned to them and hoisted a huge spear in the air, its iron tip alone weighing 15 pounds.

When he turned back to Israel, there was fury in his eyes. "This day I defy the armies of Israel!" he shouted. "Give me a man and let us fight each other" (17:10).

In terror, Israel fled.

David was livid. He grasped the arm of a warrior standing next to him and demanded an explanation. "What will be done for the man who kills this Philistine and removes this disgrace from Israel? Who is this uncircumcised Philistine that he should defy the armies of the living God?" (17:26).

From the safety of his tent, Saul sat with his eyes closed and listened to Goliath's mockery and blasphemy. He felt humiliated as he heard the cries of terror while his army scrambled for safety. A moment later, one of his servants cautiously parted the tent, allowing a sharp blade of offending sunlight into the dim interior. Saul winced and shielded his eyes from the glare.

"What is it?" he demanded wearily.

"My lord, there is a youth just arrived in camp who is willing to face the Philistine in battle," the servant said.

"Send him in," Saul ordered.

Saul stood and smoothed the wrinkles from his cloak and ran one hand through his disheveled hair just as the servant pulled the entrance of the tent wide and David stepped inside. He bowed low before the king. Saul looked down in disbelief. The boy, Israel's champion, wore a simple shepherd's tunic and carried a staff in his hand. A common shepherd's sling was tucked securely in his belt.

"Let no one lose heart on account of this Philistine," David said to Saul. "Your servant will go and fight him" (17:32).

Saul was aghast. "You are not able to go out against this Philistine and fight him; you are only a young man, and he has been a warrior from his youth," he said (17:33).

But David was not shaken. "Your servant has killed both the lion and the bear; this uncircumcised Philistine will be like one of them, because he has defied the armies of the living God. The LORD who rescued me from the paw of the lion and the paw of the bear will rescue me from the hand of this Philistine" (17:36–37).

For a moment Saul stared down at the boy, sensing a hint of something once familiar but now lost. Something sweet, and yet infinitely powerful. A mystery that dwelt in the wasteland between life and death, between courage and fear.

Saul saw the faintest trace of the man he once hoped to be.

"Go," Saul said softly, "and the LORD be with you" (17:37).

Saul called for his own tunic for David and a set of bronze armor. The boy donned them and strapped a sword to his waist before awkwardly stumbling about the tent.

"I cannot go in these," he said to Saul, "because I am not used to them" (17:39).

The servants helped David remove the heavy armor and handed him his staff and sling. He stepped from the tent to find the entire army silently waiting. They parted as he walked through them and headed toward the battlefield where Goliath stood waiting.

David stood atop the hill for a moment, looking down at his formidable foe, then ran down the slope and into the valley. He paused at the stream that ran through the valley and carefully chose five smooth stones before adding them to the shepherd's pouch that was tied to his belt.

Then the shepherd boy, the secret true king of Israel, walked purposefully toward the Philistine giant. Goliath wore a bronze helmet, fringed with feathers. Bronze armor shielded his chest, and bronze greaves wrapped his legs from knee to ankle. In addition to the massive spear in his hand, he carried a bronze javelin slung on his back and a sword at his belt.

Goliath squinted as the slim figure approached and then he began to howl in laughter at the sight of Israel's champion—a mere boy with a shepherd's staff in one hand and a sling in the other.

"Am I a dog, that you come at me with sticks?" Goliath shouted at David. "Come here, and I'll give your flesh to the birds and the wild animals!" (17:43–44).

David's eyes flashed in anger. "You come against me with sword and spear and javelin," he shouted at Goliath, "but I come against you in the name of the LORD Almighty, the God of the armies of Israel, whom you have defied. This day the LORD will deliver you into my hands, and I'll strike you down and cut off your head…and the whole world will know that there is a God in Israel" (17:45–46).

David then ran toward Goliath, pulling a stone from his pouch and putting it into the center of his sling. With practiced ease he began swinging the sling around and around in a huge arc, gaining momentum with each rotation. And then, he let the string go.

The stone tore through the air at over one hundred miles per hour and found its mark just beneath the bronze band of Goliath's helmet. The huge warrior stumbled and then fell face down into the dust, dead, with David's last words still ringing in his ears.

"All those gathered here will know that it is not by sword or spear that the LORD saves; for the battle is the LORD's, and He will give all of you into our hands" (17:47).

David stood over Goliath for a moment before bending over to pull the Philistine's sword from its sheath. With trembling arms, he lifted the heavy weapon high into the air. Then, with a shout of victory, he let it fall as the Philistine army fled and Israel's warriors poured into the valley in pursuit.

Father,

How often have I fallen into despair, believing that the battle before me depends on my own strength and resources? As You did for Your servant David, empower me to boldly refuse to limit my hope for the future based on the meager provisions in my hands.

Help me carry the hope of Advent with me today, resting in the truth that though my path is dark at times, the promise of the Baby in the manger is ever bright. Though I am weak and my enemy is mighty, the battle remains Yours always.

Amen

Wise and Foolish

DAVID   SOLOMON   ELIJAH

THE KING, MOREOVER, MUST NOT ACQUIRE
GREAT NUMBERS OF HORSES FOR HIMSELF
OR MAKE THE PEOPLE RETURN TO
EGYPT TO GET MORE OF THEM,
FOR THE LORD HAS TOLD YOU,
"YOU ARE NOT TO GO BACK THAT WAY AGAIN."
HE MUST NOT TAKE MANY WIVES,
OR HIS HEART WILL BE LED ASTRAY.
HE MUST NOT ACCUMULATE LARGE
AMOUNTS OF SILVER AND GOLD.

DEUTERONOMY 17:16–17

YOU SHALL HAVE NO OTHER
GODS BEFORE ME.

EXODUS 20:3

As the evening sun dropped lower in the sky, long shadows crept across the palace floor. Silently, servants entered the king's private chambers and lit the lamps one by one.

Solomon's eyes never left his father, David, watching as his chest rose and fell. As the day stretched into evening, so did the pauses between one breath and the next. With each inhalation and exhalation, Solomon pondered his father's final instructions, gifts of wisdom from one king to the next, on how to lead Israel well.

Be strong, show yourself a man... Walk in the ways of the Lord... Keep his decrees and commands... Walk faithfully before the Lord with all our heart and soul...

The room grew darker still as Solomon took his father's hand in his. A hand that had fought bears and lions. A hand that had once slain a giant. A hand that had written poetry, played music, and conquered kingdoms. Now, David's hand felt as frail and weightless as a child's as it rested in Solomon's.

Solomon pressed his cheek against the back of David's hand and stifled a sob as the king after God's own heart sighed softly in his sleep.

And breathed no more.

Solomon stood atop Gibeon as the priests attended the brass altar of the Lord where the last of one thousand sacrifices turned to ashes. Behind the priests rose the tabernacle commissioned by Moses in the wilderness. A gust of wind caught the smoke from the sacrifice and drove it toward the tabernacle, temporarily enshrouding it.

As the smoke lifted, Solomon watched as the goat-hair covering trembled in the breeze. The stakes tethering the tent to the ground held firm. For generations, God had met Israel there. Now, Solomon knew, that season was drawing to a close. His father, David, had gathered the supplies and drawn up the architectural plans for a temple before his death. It was Solomon's destiny to build it not from a state of war as in David's time, but from a heart of peace as in Solomon's.

With the last sacrifice consumed, Solomon left the priests to attend the dying embers of the fire. The long day was drawing to a close and he ached for the comfort of his tent.

Solomon sighed with relief as he ducked inside the tent flaps to find lamps softly burning and his evening meal of couscous with yogurt, olives, bread, and wine waiting for him on a rug in the center of the tent. He washed his hands in the basin by the door and sat down on the floor to eat.

Once he finished his meal and drained the last sweet drops of wine from the cup, he extinguished the lamps, crawled into bed, and fell asleep.

And there atop Gibeon, where the aroma of one thousand sacrifices still lingered in the night air, God met Solomon in his dreams.

"Ask for whatever you want Me to give you," God said to Solomon (I Kings 3:5).

"LORD my God," Solomon answered, "You have made Your servant king in place of my father David. But I am only a little child and do not know how to carry out my duties. Your servant is here among the people You have chosen, a great people too numerous to count or number. So give Your servant a discerning heart to govern Your people and to distinguish between right and wrong" (3:7–9).

Solomon's request was beautiful to God, and He granted Solomon such wisdom that all the kings and queens surrounding Israel came to Solomon to learn from him. The king studied plants and fauna, wrote extensively, and rendered brilliant judgments to settle the disputes of his people.

King Solomon built God's temple and filled it with furnishings of pure gold.

God granted Solomon wealth and power as well. Solomon constructed his own sprawling palace complex, expanded Israel's territory, fortified key cities, and formed strong diplomatic alliances with Israel's neighbors. Every three years, Israel's ships pulled into port heavily laden with gold, silver, and exotic animals. Wealth flowed so freely in Israel's streets that silver was "as common in Jerusalem as stones" (10:27).

But for all of his wisdom, success, and renown, the king had a fatal flaw. Like a deadly poison, delivered one drop at a time, this moral weakness seeped into Solomon's life, infected his rule, and ultimately spread throughout Israel with plague-like efficiency.

Solomon "loved many foreign women" (11:1). Eventually, he grew to love their gods too.

Solomon knew well God's warnings to Israel against marrying women from other lands who worshiped other gods. He remembered his father David's final charge that obedience to God's law was the firm foundation upon which his kingdom would rise secure.

But Solomon cast aside the wisdom of God to trust in his own judgment. In an effort to strengthen Israel's relationship with her allies, he entered into a treaty with Egypt and sealed it by taking Pharaoh's daughter as his wife.

As the years slipped by and new threats arose on Israel's borders, Solomon secured his kingdom through more treaties. With each treaty came a new princess, until his harem overflowed with beautiful women of royal blood. Ultimately, Solomon married seven hundred princesses and took three hundred concubines from foreign lands.

And Solomon loved them all.

Boom. Boom. Boom.

The royal procession slowly made its way out of Jerusalem and up the hillside to the east where worshipers were already striking the massive drums surrounding the altar. There, a statue of Chemosh The Destroyer, fish-god of Moab, waited with arms outstretched to receive its offering.

Boom. Boom. Boom.

The drums called to the throng as it ascended, and the fire at Chemosh's feet crackled and leapt, hungry for prey.

Enrobed in fine linen of scarlet and purple, Solomon's many wives climbed, carrying their royal babies in their arms. Pure gold glittered in the fierce sunlight as it dangled from their wrists, arms, and noses, draped around their necks, and encircled their foreheads. There in their midst, climbing alongside them, was the gray head of the king...

The king who once had offered one thousand sacrifices at the tabernacle to the one true God. The king who asked God for wisdom and received it, along with greater riches than he could have ever imagined. The king to whom the nations paid tribute and to whom kings and queens turned for guidance.

Wise King Solomon, foolishly blind to the most fatal of flaws, until it was too late.

The procession crested the hill and encircled Chemosh. As the first princess lifted her child into The Destroyer's arms, the drums roared, drowning out the baby's anguished cries.

But God heard.

"Since this is your attitude and you have not kept My covenant and My decrees, which I commanded you," God said to Solomon, *"I will most certainly tear the kingdom away from you and give it to one of your subordinates. Nevertheless, for the sake of David your father, I will not do it during your lifetime. I will tear it out of the hand of your son. Yet I will not tear the whole kingdom from him, but will give him one tribe for the sake of David My servant and for the sake of Jerusalem, which I have chosen"* (11:11–13).

Years passed as kingdoms rose and fell. Centuries after the last of the sacrificial fires burned to ashes and the cries of the innocent faded, Israel's sons and daughters settled on the hill. They planted lush gardens and shady olive groves and named it...the Mount of Olives.

And there, where God's people once offered their own children in the fires of idolatrous worship, the Son of God wept. His tears, mixed with blood, fell onto the sin-cursed earth as He wrestled in prayer that Passover night. Beneath the silvery olive leaves of the garden of Gethsemane, the spotless Lamb of God prepared Himself as a sacrifice to take away the sins of the world.

Wondrous Savior,

In the darkest night of our violence and cruelty, when Eden's glory and purpose had long been forgotten, You came.

You came to restore and renew, to heal our wounds, to remind us who we are. There on the sin-scarred Mount of Olives, stained with Your wisest king's most poisonous flaw, You shed blood-soaked tears of redemption for all humanity.

This season, as the riches of this world clamor for my affection, remind me that my greatest gift forever remains wrapped in the rags of a peasant and resting in a manger.

Amen

The Lord, He Is God

ELIJAH

WHAT FAULT DID YOUR ANCESTORS FIND IN ME,
THAT THEY STRAYED SO FAR FROM ME?
THEY FOLLOWED WORTHLESS IDOLS
AND BECAME WORTHLESS THEMSELVES.
I BROUGHT YOU INTO A FERTILE LAND
TO EAT ITS FRUIT AND RICH PRODUCE.
BUT YOU CAME AND DEFILED MY LAND
AND MADE MY INHERITANCE DETESTABLE.
THE PRIESTS DID NOT ASK,
"WHERE IS THE LORD?"
THOSE WHO DEAL WITH THE LAW DID NOT KNOW ME;
THE LEADERS REBELLED AGAINST ME.
THE PROPHETS PROPHESIED BY BAAL,
FOLLOWING WORTHLESS IDOLS.

JEREMIAH 2:5, 7–8

Is that you, you troubler of Israel?" King Ahab called to Elijah the prophet (I Kings 18:17).

The two men walked toward each other across a landscape so desiccated that deep cracks snaked across the dusty ground. Barren fig and olive trees once lush with vegetation lifted skeletal limbs to a pale and cloudless sky.

The sun glared down mercilessly. As Elijah and Ahab drew near each other, they instinctively ducked into the shade of a rock outcropping on the hillside above them. It had been three years since they last met on the day Elijah threw open the doors of Ahab's ivory palace to deliver God's message of judgment: Not one drop of rain would fall on Israel until Elijah gave the word.

God was weary of Israel's idolatry with the Canaanite fertility god, Baal. It was time to show His children beyond all doubt that He alone was the one who controlled the rainfall Israel so desperately needed for her crops.

The king, robed in linen richly dyed with purple, scarlet, and blue, leaned against the hillside, crossed his arms, and glared sullenly at the prophet before him. Elijah stepped forward, closing the distance between the two men until they were almost nose to nose. The king's face paled as he stared into the prophet's dark eyes, narrowed in fury. Above them, Elijah's black, wiry eyebrows knit together. His beard was long. His wild hair just brushed the shoulders of a mantle of woven camel's hair. When he spoke, his voice was low and dangerous.

"I have not made trouble for Israel," Elijah replied. "But you and your father's family have. You have abandoned the LORD's commands and have followed the Baals. Now summon the people from all over Israel to meet me on Mount Carmel. And bring the four hundred and fifty prophets of Baal and the four hundred prophets of Asherah, who eat at Jezebel's table" (18:18–19).

Then, without awaiting a response, the prophet turned to make his way up the mountaintop.

Once he arrived, Elijah walked to the center of a clearing. The prophets of Baal clustered together at one end of the open space, waiting for God's prophet to make the first move. The Israelites encircled the site, chatting excitedly and jostling each other to get a clearer view of the contest unfolding before them.

Elijah raised his hand and the crowd quieted.

"I am the only one of the LORD's prophets left, but Baal has four hundred and fifty prophets," Elijah shouted to the vast crowd. "Get two bulls for us. Let Baal's prophets choose one for themselves, and let them cut it into pieces and put it on the wood but not set fire to it. I will prepare the other bull and put it on the wood but not set fire to it. Then you call on the name of your god, and I will call on the name of the LORD. The god who answers by fire—he is God" (18:22–24).

The people agreed to the challenge as Elijah turned to offer the prophets of Baal the opportunity to call on their god first. The men slapped each other on the shoulders, laughing with all confidence. This prophet before them was not only outnumbered, he was challenging them in the place they felt the most powerful.

Mount Carmel, known for its lush vegetation and abundant rainfall, was an important worship center for the prophets of Baal. Once, long ago, an altar to the God of Israel had stood on the mountain, but it had long since fallen into ruins. Now Mount Carmel belonged to Baal, and his prophets knew it.

Once the bull was laid upon the altar, the prophets began dancing around it and shouting for Baal to rain down fire on their sacrifice. As the morning sun climbed higher into the sky, they danced more frantically and shouted ever louder. At last, they began cutting themselves with swords and spears in an effort to rouse their god to action.

But there was no response.

As the sun dipped low in the sky, Elijah called the people of Israel closer.

"Come to me," he said to them.

Then he walked over to the weed-strewn pile of rubble that had once been the altar of the Lord. He gathered twelve stones, one for each of the twelve tribes of Israel, and carefully laid them one on top of the other. As the people watched, he dug a deep trench all around the altar. Finally, he piled the wood for the sacrifice on the stones, cut the bull into sections, and laid it on top.

Elijah stepped back, dusted off his hands, and surveyed his work before turning to some men standing nearby. "Fill four large jars with water and pour it on the offering and on the wood," he said (18:33).

The exhausted prophets of Baal lifted their weary heads in hope. True, they had failed, but surely Elijah would fail as well. It was difficult enough to call down fire from heaven, but for some reason he was making the situation impossible by drenching the sacrifice with water.

The men returned with large clay jars of water balanced on their shoulders. They poured them over the sacrifice. The water sloshed over the bull and ran down the sides of the altar, soaking immediately into the thirsty wood and stones.

"Do it again," Elijah instructed (18:34).

A murmur of disbelief swept through the crowd. Soon, the men returned to empty their jars of water on the sacrifice once again.

"Do it a third time," Elijah said (18:34).

As the men turned to fill their water jugs for a third time, the prophets of Baal stood to their feet, encouraged by the impossibility of the challenge before Elijah.

For the last time, the men emptied their jugs of water onto the sacrifice, soaking it and even filling the trench at its base. At that moment, the traditional time for Israel's evening sacrifice to God drew near. Elijah stepped in front of the sacrifice and lifted his face and hands to heaven.

"LORD, the God of Abraham, Isaac and Israel, let it be known today that You are God in Israel and that I am Your servant and have done all these things at Your command. Answer me, LORD, answer me, so these people will know that You, LORD, are God, and that You are turning their hearts back again" (18:36–37).

A blinding flash of light split the evening sky with a deafening crack, followed by a brilliant column of white lightning so hot that it consumed the bull, wood, water, and even the stones of the altar and the soil surrounding it.

The people cried out in terror and fell trembling to the ground, pressing their faces into the dust.

"The LORD—He is God!" "The LORD—He is God!" the people cried (18:39).

But Elijah knew Israel's confession wasn't enough. She had to remove the disease of idolatry from her land.

"Seize the prophets of Baal," Elijah said to the people. "Don't let anyone get away!" (18:40).

Then the prophet turned to ashen-faced King Ahab.

"Go, eat and drink," he said to the king as he looked up into a cloudless sky where a full moon was just rising, "for there is the sound of a heavy rain" (18:41).

Creator of all,

You alone are God and worthy of my devotion. Forgive me for the times my faith wanes and idolatry rules. May I be continually aware of the struggle and thankful for the covering of Your grace. Let my heart cry out with all of creation: The Lord—He is God!

Amen

The Sound of Rain

SOLOMON

ELIJAH

JOSIAH

THE ISRAELITES PERSISTED IN ALL
THE SINS OF JEROBOAM
AND DID NOT TURN AWAY FROM THEM
UNTIL THE LORD REMOVED THEM FROM HIS PRESENCE,
AS HE HAD WARNED THROUGH
ALL HIS SERVANTS THE PROPHETS.
SO THE PEOPLE OF ISRAEL WERE TAKEN
FROM THEIR HOMELAND
INTO EXILE IN ASSYRIA,
AND THEY ARE STILL THERE.

II KINGS 17:22–23

L et's go," Elijah said to his servant before turning to take one last look at King Ahab.

The full moon was so bright that the king had no need of a lamp to light the simple meal his servants had prepared for him. He sat on the ground on the mountainside, a colorful rug between him and the dusty earth. He ate quickly. He had spent a long day on Mount Carmel, standing witness to the vain attempts of the prophets of Baal to coax their god into raining down fire upon their sacrifice. He was hungry and tired.

And he was in no hurry to tell his wife, Jezebel, that her prophets not only failed but were now dead. After God rained fire from heaven onto Elijah's sacrifice, the people were all too eager to litter the valley below with the bodies of the defeated prophets. No, he was just fine with eating his meal on the peaceful mountainside instead of at the palace with Jezebel. He would be forced to give her the news soon enough, and she would be furious.

Elijah turned onto the path before him and took his first step toward the summit. He was weak with hunger and exhausted too, but there was still work left to do this night. After a moment, he and his servant fell into a companionable silence as they faced the demands of the trail leading upward. One foot in front of the other. Stone, by stone, by stone.

At last, with hearts pounding from the grueling climb, the pair reached the rock-strewn summit. Elijah reached up to wipe away a bead of sweat that trickled into his eye. A dry cough caught in his servant's throat, irritated by the dust that rose into the still, dry air. The mountaintop was baked to a crisp, desiccated by the relentless sun and recalcitrant rain.

Briefly, the pair stood looking out over the Mediterranean Sea reflecting the moonlight. The sky was perfectly clear.

Elijah dropped wearily to the ground and bent forward until his face rested between his knees and his beard swept the dust beneath him.

"Oh, God...let it rain. Let it rain. Let it rain..." he prayed.

Elijah stopped praying after a moment, sat back on his heels, and turned to the young man accompanying him. "Go, look out over the sea in every direction. See if there is any sign of rain."

The servant rushed along the edge of the cliff, scanning the horizon. He desperately hoped for great rolling masses of dark storm clouds and a sea churning with whitecaps from the approaching gale, but the water remained deathly still. The sky was barren. When he returned to Elijah, his eyes were downcast.

"There is nothing there," he said (I Kings 18:43).

Elijah bowed and prayed again. *"Let it rain..."*

Again, he sent the servant to look for rain. When the young man returned, his voice was tainted with despair.

"There is nothing..."

Six times, Elijah prayed. Six times, the servant returned to report cloudless skies and calm seas.

Then, Elijah bowed low, pressing his face to the dust one more time. When the servant gazed out to the sea the seventh time, there was no lightning, no thunder, no mighty, fearsome wind. But... illuminated beneath the moonlight was a tiny cloud floating above the water. He scanned the sky above the sea for any other sign, but there was nothing. For a moment he watched as the small cloud climbed higher in the night sky and drifted in front of the radiant moon. Then he returned to Elijah.

"There is a cloud as small as a man's hand rising out of the sea," he said to his master.

Elijah scrambled to his feet. "Quickly then, on your way," he said to his servant. "Tell Ahab, 'Saddle up and get down from the mountain before the rain stops you'" (18:44 THE MESSAGE).

Second by second, the tiny cloud grew and darkened as Elijah followed his servant down the mountain. The wind began to howl, rattling the dry tree limbs overhead and whipping the dusty earth into a wall of grime that stung their eyes and coated their hair and skin.

Down below, Ahab jumped into his chariot as the now black clouds swirled overhead. With a crack of Ahab's whip, the horses bolted forward as the first drops of rain drummed onto the parched earth.

Elijah reached the bottom of the mountain, turned his face to the falling rain, and shouted toward the sky in victory. Then, filled with the awesome power of God, he tucked his robe into his belt and ran ahead of the chariot all the way back to Samaria. Behind him, the king lashed the horses, pushing them to their limit. Man and beast raced on and on, driven by the wind and the rain…

A downpour of God's grace on a sin-parched land.

Merciful God,

I, like Your daughter Israel, am prone to wander far away from Your love and protection. Thank You for calling me back to Your heart time and time again. Gently You lead me with cords of human kindness and heal my wounds. You bend low in compassion to set me free from every tangled snare.*

How can it be, my God, that You should love me so much that You sent Your precious Son to bring me home? May my heart never cease to rejoice in the hope of Advent and the good tidings of great joy You bring to all creation. Unto us a Savior is born!

Amen

*Prayer is based on God's anguished call to His child Israel, found in Hosea 11.

Good King Josiah

ELIJAH

JOSIAH

ZERUBBABEL

WHO IS A GOD LIKE YOU,
WHO PARDONS SIN AND
FORGIVES THE TRANSGRESSION
OF THE REMNANT OF HIS INHERITANCE?
YOU DO NOT STAY ANGRY FOREVER
BUT DELIGHT TO SHOW MERCY.
YOU WILL AGAIN HAVE COMPASSION ON US;
YOU WILL TREAD OUR SINS UNDERFOOT
AND HURL ALL OUR INIQUITIES INTO
THE DEPTHS OF THE SEA.
YOU WILL BE FAITHFUL TO JACOB,
AND SHOW LOVE TO ABRAHAM,
AS YOU PLEDGED ON OATH
TO OUR ANCESTORS
IN DAYS LONG AGO.

MICAH 7:18–20

Nine-year-old King Josiah bolted down the lamp-lit corridors of the palace with his nurse in hot pursuit. Every few seconds, he cast a glance over his shoulder at the portly woman's flushed cheeks and furrowed brow as she waddled along behind him, and he dissolved into giggles.

He skidded through a doorway and then bounded up the stairs two at a time, leaving the sound of the nurse's labored breath far below. Breathless with laughter, he shot toward the doorway leading to the next corridor, just as Hilkiah the priest, his faithful tutor, stepped out in front of him to block his path.

"Time for bed, I think," Hilkiah said with a small smile. "Come, I will tell you a story."

The frustrated nurse reached Josiah's chambers just behind the tutor and his royal charge. For a moment, she stood gasping for breath, glaring at the young king. Hilkiah smiled and dismissed her with a small wave as Josiah jumped into bed.

"Tell me the story about when God parted the sea!" he begged.

"Yes, the sea," Hilkiah said as he patted the bed and reached for the blanket at the end. Reluctantly, Josiah lay down at last as his tutor pulled the blanket up beneath the boy's chin.

"And don't forget the part about Pharaoh!" Josiah said.

Hilkiah reached up to gently smooth the boy-king's curls. The child was so close to the age of his own son, yet so much was at stake in his reign. What kind of king would he be? Would he follow after God like his great-grandfather Hezekiah, or would he follow after false gods like his grandfather and father?

And so, Hilkiah gave Josiah the best chance he could: he told him stories. This night, he told King Josiah the story of how the Creator of the universe loved Israel, and of how, when her cries reached His ears from her Egyptian bondage, He forced Pharaoh to let His people go. He told Josiah of how God held back the walls of the sea so that His people could cross safely, and then let the water rush back when Pharaoh and his chariots followed in pursuit.

The child's eyes grew heavy and then closed, the rhythmic rise and fall of his chest signaling that one more day in shaping the young king's heart had come to a close. Hilkiah rose, took the oil lamp from its stand, and moved silently to the door, where armed guards stood ready to protect the boy. Hilkiah paused for a moment, turned, and whispered an ancient prayer over the child and all of Judah.

"The LORD bless you and keep you; the LORD make his face shine on you and be gracious to you; the LORD turn his face toward you and give you peace" (Numbers 6:24–26).

Twenty-six-year-old King Josiah sat on a gilded throne, inlaid with ivory. For ten years, he had reigned over Judah independently, finally old enough to rule apart from his trusted advisors. For the past six years, he had begun working to reform many of the idolatrous practices promoted by his father and grandfather. Finally, he had enough funds to begin a much-needed restoration of the temple. Now he eagerly awaited an update on the efforts from his trusted secretary, Shaphan.

The distinguished official swept into the room carrying a large scroll and bowed low before the king. "Your officials have paid out the money that was in the temple of the LORD and have entrusted it to the workers and supervisors at the temple," Shaphan said (II Kings 22:9).

King Josiah smiled and nodded. The work on the temple could begin at last.

"Also," Shaphan said, "while cleaning at the temple, Hilkiah the priest found something that seems to be important. It is a book."

Josiah sat on the edge of his throne in expectation. "Please, read it to me," he said.

Shaphan unrolled the parchment, revealing line after line of neat script on the yellowing pages, and began to read from the book of the law given by Moses. The words of the Lord fell like blows, one after the other, from Shaphan's lips as he read. Josiah grew pale and gripped the arms of his throne until his knuckles turned white.

"You shall have no other gods before Me. You shall not make for yourself an image in the form of anything in heaven above or on the earth beneath or in the waters below. You shall not bow down to them or worship them; for I, the LORD your God, am a jealous God" (Deuteronomy 5:7–9).

Shaphan read on and on as the afternoon shadows grew long on the palace floors. When the last lines of the law were read, the secretary bowed his head low in horror. The king fell to his knees, grasped the top of his tunic with both hands, and ripped it in two in mourning for his people's grave sins.

Sites of pagan worship dotted Judah's landscape. Asherah poles littered every high hill. Fires burned to Molech, Topheth, and Chemosh in the valleys where ceremonial drums roared and fragile infants wailed in torment. Even the temple of the Lord had been defiled with articles of idolatrous worship. An Asherah pole stood in its sanctuary, and shelters for shrine prostitutes were clustered outside its walls.

"Go, and take Hilkiah, Ahikam, Akbor, and Asaiah with you," the king said. "Go and inquire of the LORD for me and for the people and for all Judah about what is written in this book that has been found. Great is the LORD's anger that burns against us because those who have gone before us have not obeyed the words of this book; they have not acted in accordance with all that is written there concerning us" (II Kings 22:13).

The king's delegation wove through the narrow streets of the market district, past baskets filled with jade-green olives, tethered lambs, jars of oil, and stacks of clay pots. Pigeons cooed softly in their cages as silver clinked and merchants haggled over prices. When the men reached the door of the royal tailor, they ducked inside. The wizened old man looked up from his delicate work on a priestly robe and then pointed one gnarled finger to the back of the shop where his wife, the prophetess Huldah, was waiting for them.

One after another, the men ducked into the small back room where bolts of bright cloth hung from racks on the ceiling. The space was tight and the air suffocating. In the corner, a tiny woman sat on a low stool, her gray braid peeking out from beneath her head covering. She carefully placed the needlework on which she was working into her lap and turned tear-filled eyes to the men crowded in her doorway.

"This is what the LORD, the God of Israel, says: Tell the man who sent you to me," she said. "'This is what the LORD says: I am going to bring disaster on this place and its people, according to everything written in the book the king of Judah has read. Because they have forsaken Me and burned incense to other gods and aroused My anger by all the idols their hands have made, My anger will burn against this place and will not be quenched'" (22:15–17).

She paused, lifted a cup of water to her lips, and when she continued, her voice was soft.

"Tell the king of Judah, who sent you to inquire of the LORD, 'This is what the LORD, the God of Israel, says concerning the words you heard: Because your heart was responsive and you humbled yourself before the LORD when you heard what I have spoken against this place and its people—that they would become a curse and be laid waste—and because you tore your robes and wept in My presence, I also have heard you, declares the LORD. Therefore I will gather you to your ancestors, and you will be buried in peace. Your eyes will not see all the disaster I am going to bring on this place'" (22:18–20).

King Josiah sent messengers to summon all of the elders of Judah to come to him. Then, in a somber procession, he led them up to the once beautiful temple Solomon had built for the God of Israel. Josiah stood next to one of the bronze pillars at the entrance of the temple and turned to Hilkiah the priest, who handed him the scroll. Carefully, the king unrolled the scroll and read the Word of God to the elders. When he was finished, he dedicated himself and his rule to the covenant of the Lord, promising to keep God's commands. After the elders also dedicated themselves to keep the covenant of the Lord, Josiah returned the scroll to Hilkiah the priest.

He stood for a moment, surveying the temple defiled with idols and the nearby quarters of the male shrine prostitutes, as his jaw clenched in fury.

"Cleanse the temple," he said to Hilkiah. "Remove every idol and every item used in worship of Baal and Asherah, and destroy them."

Josiah burned everything associated with idolatrous worship and scattered the ashes. He tore down the shelters of the shrine prostitutes and drove the priests of Baal from the temple. Then, methodically, he moved from one site of idolatrous worship throughout Judah to the next, cleansing his land.

One morning, he and his soldiers climbed the Mount of Olives to stand before a shrine to Chemosh The Destroyer that had held dominion over the hillside since the time of Solomon.

Josiah stood before the fish-god, its stony arms outstretched to receive its sacrifices. The base of the statue was black with the ashes of a thousand fires. The anguished cries of countless children seemed to haunt the place, lingering in the soft rustling of silvery olive leaves.

With a nod from the king, his men moved in. They tied a heavy rope around the base of the statue. The other end was tethered to an ox. The driver of the ox cried out, and the beast moved forward. With a groan, Chemosh crashed to the ground.

When the land was finally cleansed from idolatry, King Josiah called his people together to celebrate Passover. They roasted spot-less lambs and ate bitter herbs with unleavened bread as the priests told the sweet story—*their* story—once again.

They told the story of how the God of the universe had loved Israel and had chosen to make them a people of His very own. How He blessed their father Abraham so that all of the nations of the earth might be blessed through him. They told of their ancestors' cruel bondage in Egypt and how God forced Pharaoh to let His people go. They told the story of how God held back the walls of the sea so His people could cross on dry land.

And how God led His people home...just as He promised.

Compassionate Father,

My heart sings with joy as I remember the stories of Your deliverance of Israel. Forever You remained faithful to Your promises to Abraham. Even when Your people strayed far from Your purposes, You mercifully preserved a remnant.

May this Advent season remind me of the hope I have in You, that though my way at times seems long and dark, Your redemption is as sure as the promise of the dawn. Rise in my heart anew, Root and Offspring of David. Shine forever bright in my darkness, beautiful Morning Star.

Amen

(Portions of this prayer are drawn from Jesus's words in Revelation 22:16.)

Songs of Joy: A Remnant Returns

JOSIAH

ZERUBBABEL

ZECHARIAH & ELIZABETH

BY THE RIVERS OF BABYLON
WE SAT AND WEPT
WHEN WE REMEMBERED ZION.
PSALM 137:1

WHEN THE LORD RESTORED
THE FORTUNES OF ZION,
WE WERE LIKE THOSE WHO DREAMED.
OUR MOUTHS WERE FILLED WITH LAUGHTER,
OUR TONGUES WITH SONGS OF JOY.
THOSE WHO SOW WITH TEARS
WILL REAP WITH SONGS OF JOY.
THOSE WHO GO OUT WEEPING,
CARRYING SEED TO SOW,
WILL RETURN WITH SONGS OF JOY,
CARRYING SHEAVES WITH THEM.
PSALM 126:1–2, 5–6

Zerubbabel, a prince of the tribe of Judah, turned to look at the long caravan stretching out behind him. Forty-two thousand, three hundred sixty men and women. Camels, horses, mules, and donkeys. Carts laden with clothing, clay pots, spoons, and kneading boards...all the mundane but necessary trappings of a home.

Still other carts were heavy with treasure, including all the gold furnishings that had been taken from the temple of God in Jerusalem by the Babylonians seventy years before.

Seventy years. When Israel went into Babylonian exile, God promised a limit to their suffering. In seventy years, He would bring them home. As the decades counted down, the fulfillment of God's promise seemed impossible. Then, as year 70 grew near, the Babylonian Empire crumbled with staggering suddenness, opening the door for a new superpower: Assyria.

Whereas Babylon's empirical strategy was total domination, Persians preferred a softer touch. In Assyria's opinion, happy subjects were compliant subjects. Almost overnight, Babylon's many captives found themselves free to return to their countries, rebuild their homes and places of worship, and rekindle devotion to their gods.

When Cyrus, king of Assyria, issued a decree allowing Abraham's people to return home, almost fifty thousand exiles answered the call.

Zerubbabel turned his attention away from his people and toward the horizon where beautiful Jerusalem once reigned. He could hear the excited chatter behind him as the caravan drew closer, but as the ruined gates of the city came into focus, the exiles fell silent.

The massive walls of Jerusalem they remembered now spilled down the hillside and into the valley below, carrying with them any hope of security for the weary travelers. Zerubbabel guided his people through the eerily silent streets. Once beautiful homes stood ghost-like, reduced to charred shells. A rat scurried in the shadows as the howl of a jackal echoed mournfully through the deserted market district.

Zerubbabel led the sorrowful procession upward, straight to the sacred ground where the temple once stood. At last, he took the final steps to stand where Solomon had once welcomed all of Israel in joyful celebration as he dedicated the temple he built for the Lord. The work of exquisite craftmanship covered with beautiful gold overlay had risen up to heaven; now it was only a heap of charred stones. Nothing was left.

Zerubbabel stood motionless, staring at the destruction as his people gathered behind him on the top of the hill. Tears flowed down his face. When the last of the exiles filled in the edges of the crowd, one man stepped forward. He placed a pot on the ground before the ruins and dropped a handful of silver inside.

Then another man approached with his family's offering. Then another, and another. The temple would rise again.

In the seventh month after the exiles had the chance to return to their towns and begin the long process of resettlement, the remnant reassembled before the ruins of the temple. Once tear-stained faces now bore traces of fear. God's people had returned home with Cyrus's blessing, but Israel's powerful enemies were determined to stop any attempts to rebuild Jerusalem.

Jerusalem's walls were destroyed, the city burned. She was weak. Vulnerable. Defenseless. Human wisdom most certainly demanded that the city's fortifications receive first priority, but the wisdom of God was calling His children back to a lesson they had learned, and forgotten, over and over again.

The only sure provision, the only fail-safe protection, was found in God alone.

"And I Myself will be a wall of fire around it [Jerusalem]," declared the Lord to His terrified people, *"and I will be its glory within"* (Zechariah 2:5–6).

Israel was determined that this time she would get it right. This time, her people would obey. They would worship first, foremost, and always.

This time, they would trust in the one and only true God.

The remnant gathered before the ruins of the temple, casting anxious eyes to the surrounding landscape where it seemed deadly enemies hid behind every tree and stone. Then, with trembling hands, the priests picked up charred stones from ruins of the altar of the Lord and stacked one upon the other.

And there, surrounded by destruction, with enemies on every side, the priests sacrificed to the Lord.

Morning and night as the years dawned and faded away, they sacrificed. The aroma from the altar rose to God as, stone by stone, the temple was rebuilt. The walls of Jerusalem were restored, and life returned to her streets.

The flames burned on as kingdoms rose and fell. The rule of Assyria gave way to the Greeks. The Greeks were driven from Israel's borders by the Maccabees, a family of rural priests who became kings and queens. As the era of the Maccabees drew to a close, Rome swept into power in Palestine and placed a puppet king on Israel's throne, an Idumean named Herod the Great.

The priesthood in Jerusalem became corrupt under Herod as the wealthy bought their way into positions of power. Many from the *true* priestly line, intent on remaining faithful to God, moved away from Jerusalem. Among these was the family of a young girl named Mary. She was betrothed to be married to Joseph, a peasant carpenter and descendant of King David. Mary and her espoused husband lived in the tiny town of Nazareth in lower Galilee.

Morning and night, the sweet aroma of sacrifices rose to heaven as the iron fist of Roman oppression tightened and the faithful once again began crying out to God for a deliverer...

A *Messiah*, to set her free.

Savior,

In the fullness of time You came, bringing deliverance greater than that from the oppression of any earthly kingdom. In the same hands that scattered the stars in the heavens and molded Adam from the earth, You held the keys of sin, hell, and death—the long-promised redemption of all creation.

Remind me, Emmanuel, that the deliverance You have planned for me is always far more beautiful than any I could ever imagine. Grant me the courage to remain faithful to You as I wait, trusting that those who go out weeping will return with songs of joy.

Amen

The Wait

THE STORY *of* ZECHARIAH

AND ELIZABETH

ZERUBBABEL

ZECHARIAH
& ELIZABETH

MARY

"I WILL SEND MY MESSENGER,
WHO WILL PREPARE THE WAY BEFORE ME.
THEN SUDDENLY THE LORD
YOU ARE SEEKING WILL COME TO HIS TEMPLE;
THE MESSENGER OF THE COVENANT,
WHOM YOU DESIRE, WILL COME,"
SAYS THE LORD ALMIGHTY.
MALACHI 3:1

Zechariah began his descent down the carved stone steps of the *mikvah*. Oil lamps nestled into recesses in the temple wall cast a soft, wavering light illuminating the passageway. Still, Zechariah moved slowly, stiffly, carefully. How many times had he walked this path over the years in the predawn silence? Year after year when his family's priestly division was called to their week of service in the temple, they made the journey to Jerusalem. For one week they lived and served there. Each and every day began in the darkest hour just before dawn in the waters of the mikvah.

Zechariah's feet dipped into the water and he descended step by step until the water rose to his chest. He lowered himself until he was completely submerged. He stood up again and began to climb a second stairway out of the mikvah.

Water dripped from his long gray hair and beard as he slipped the first of his priestly garments over his head. Once dressed, he and his priestly brethren each grasped a torch and filed into the temple courts. Half of the group proceeded eastward, the other half westward, inspecting the temple as they walked. When they met in the middle on the other end, they made their way into the Hall of Polished Stones where they would cast lots to divide the tasks for the day.

Zechariah and his fellow priests formed a circle around the head priest. Once everyone was in place, the head priest removed the headpiece of one of the priests as a signal that he would begin counting with him. After this, each priest held up either one or two fingers, and the head priest called out the number he had chosen for the lots. Beginning with the chosen priest, he began counting around the circle. When he reached his chosen number, that priest was assigned the first duty: to cleanse the altar. The head priest repeated the process twice more. The priest chosen by the second lot was assigned the duty of cleansing the altar of incense and the candlestick in the Holy Place. The third and last duty chosen by lot was the most precious of all. It determined the priest who would offer incense in the Holy Place. The service was such an honor that, once a priest was chosen, he was disqualified from all future consideration.

And this day, after so many years of longing and waiting, the third lot landed on Zechariah.

By mid-morning, at the Hour of Incense, the temple courts were filled with worshipers. Zechariah stood before the door of the Holy Place cradling the dish of incense in his hands that symbolized the prayers of the people. As he stepped from the bright morning sun into the dim interior of the Holy Place, the crowd outside began to pray. Zechariah took slow, reverent steps toward the altar of incense. He stood over the glowing embers, dipped his fingers into the fragrant incense, and sprinkled it into the fire. The smell of the incense intensified and the smoke drifted heavenward as the prayers of the worshippers outside rose to God.

Zechariah knew what it meant to pray. For years and years he and his wife, Elizabeth, had asked God for a child. Decades passed and they both grew old, but God had not answered. Now Zechariah stood before the altar of incense and found that his prayers had grown faint by the anguished years of God's silence.

Suddenly, the space was filled with the brilliance of the noonday sun. Zechariah gasped and stumbled backward. Once his eyes adjusted to the glare, he found there was an angel standing to the right of the altar. The angel was tall and powerful. His robes shimmered with light.

"Do not be afraid, Zechariah," the angel said; "your prayer has been heard. Your wife Elizabeth will bear you a son, and you are to call him John. He will be a joy and delight to you, and many will rejoice because of his birth, for he will be great in the sight of the Lord.... He will be filled with the Holy Spirit even before he is born" (Luke 1:13–15).

The angel told Zechariah that his son would serve God in the same spirit of Elijah. His birth was destined for that very moment in time, for he was the forerunner of the Messiah.

But the wait had cost Zechariah. His heart was so battered and his faith worn so thin that he struggled to believe his most precious of prayers had been answered, even when the good news was hand-delivered by angelic announcement in front of the altar of incense. When he spoke, his voice was barely above a whisper, his head bowed in sorrow and doubt.

"How can I be sure of this?" Zechariah asked the angel. "I am an old man and my wife is well along in years."

"I am Gabriel," the angel said to Zechariah. "I stand in the presence of God, and I have been sent to speak to you and to bring you this good news. And now you will be silent and not able to speak until the day this happens, because you did not believe my words, which will come true at their appointed time" (1:19–20).

Then, as suddenly as he appeared, Gabriel was gone and the room plunged into shadows and flickering firelight once again. Zechariah's hand trembled as he pulled the incense bowl to his chest. With the other hand, he felt his way along the wall and out into daylight to face the worshipers.

Zechariah returned home to Elizabeth, and after what seemed a lifetime of waiting, she conceived a child. The months passed slowly, but this time the wait was different. It was heavy with expectation and Zechariah's silent wonder at the fidelity of God.

Eight days after Elizabeth gave birth, Zechariah stood cradling his infant son on the day of the child's circumcision. His friends, family, and neighbors gathered around him, eager to know the baby's name. Silent Zechariah sat down, balanced his writing tablet on his knee, and scrawled the name the angel had given him in the Holy Place.

"His name is John," he wrote.

Immediately, Zechariah's voice returned to him. The long months of silence were over. As the baby quieted and drifted off to sleep on his father's shoulder, Zechariah lifted his voice in praise to the God for whom nothing was impossible. The new father brushed his gray beard across the top of his baby's head with a kiss.

John, son of Zechariah. The baby who was born to prepare the way for the Messiah. The baby who wasn't late after all. The baby who was right on time.

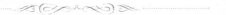

Faithful God,

I am so often impatient for You. With suffering Job, I rail against the doors of heaven, begging for deliverance. Like Zechariah, I grow weary in prayer when Your answer tarries. With the psalmist I cry, "I am forgotten" (Psalm 31:12).

But You remember me, O God. You bend Your ear from heaven to hear my cry. You keep my tears in Your bottle. You, O Faithful One, move steadily, purposefully, throughout the corridors of time.

Have mercy on me in my weakness. Give me strength to hope anew in Your unfailing love. Help me trust that Your answers are always on time.

Amen

Betrothal

DO NOT LET YOUR HEARTS BE TROUBLED.

YOU BELIEVE IN GOD; BELIEVE ALSO IN ME.

MY FATHER'S HOUSE HAS MANY ROOMS;

IF THAT WERE NOT SO,

WOULD I HAVE TOLD YOU THAT I AM GOING

THERE TO PREPARE A PLACE FOR YOU?

AND IF I GO AND PREPARE A PLACE FOR YOU,

I WILL COME BACK

AND TAKE YOU TO BE WITH ME

THAT YOU ALSO MAY BE WHERE I AM.

JOHN 14:1–3

The sweet notes of a lyre rose and fell as a tambourine kept rhythm and the voices of the harvesters swelled with songs of praise.

> May the peoples praise You, God;
> may all the peoples praise You.
> The land yields its harvest;
> God, our God, blesses us.
> May God bless us still!

Thirteen-year-old Mary tossed her head back and laughed as she held tightly to her cousins hands. Round and round they marched and danced in the winepress, keeping rhythm with the music, their bare feet popping open the grapes beneath them.

She scanned the faces of the joyful villagers, each familiar and so very dear to her heart. But Mary's eyes longed for one face alone.

Then, there he was, stepping through the rock wall surrounding the winepress, holding a basket of grapes on his shoulder. He set it down with the other grapes awaiting the press. Then he looked up, his eyes met Mary's, and he smiled.

Mary smiled in return and felt her cheeks grow hot.

Joseph. Sweet, handsome Joseph. Mary had known Joseph all of her life. In a town as small as Nazareth, everyone was close. One of her earliest memories was of eight-year-old Joseph bending down to comfort her when she fell and scraped her knee as the village children played tag among the terraces of hilly Nazareth.

"Come, Mary," he had said as he wiped her tears with the sleeve of his robe. "Let me help you home to your mother."

The years passed as Mary inched toward adulthood, four years behind Joseph. He grew tall and muscular, leaving school and childish games to work alongside his father as a carpenter while Mary played games, strung together crowns of coriander, and danced with her friends hand in hand beneath the silvery olive leaves.

Then came Mary's twelfth summer and everything changed.

She didn't even notice when it happened; not at first. Perhaps it was when she was drawing water from the well or playing with her friends that deep inside her some mysterious timepiece struck midnight. Silently, powerful forces were released, setting in motion the most profound series of transformations she had experienced since she developed in her mother's womb.

Day after day her body changed, morphing into a person who was strange and new to her. Her arms and legs grew long and lanky like the coriander that crowded the fields of her play. The outlines of her body softened as sharp, boyish angles were replaced by the gentler curves of womanhood.

If her outward metamorphosis was unsettling, it paled in comparison to her inner self. Suddenly, the games she had always enjoyed seemed juvenile and silly. Her emotions stunned her, surging and dipping like the waves of the sea.

But the dramatic changes in her body and mind were just a foreshadowing of greater changes to come. Puberty meant the little girl who not so long ago had been playing childhood games was about to become a wife.

The informal negotiations between Mary's family and Joseph's had sweetened her thirteenth summer. Soon, very soon, Joseph would come to her home with their betrothal contract in his hand to formalize the engagement.

The lyrist's fingers moved faster across the strings as the villagers clapped and sang. Mary and her friends giggled breathlessly, their feet rising and falling with the beat of the music. The sweet aroma of the harvest drifted across the hillside as grape juice ran dark and sweet into the stone channel that led from the winepress to the collection vats on the lower terrace.

And Mary danced.

Joseph walked down the familiar streets of Nazareth toward Mary's home, a route he could easily have navigated blindfolded or on the darkest moonless night. But this time was different. In one hand he clutched a small pouch of silver, his bridal gift. In the other, he and Mary's *ketubah*, a legal document guaranteeing her rights in the marriage. The document, and the protections it provided Mary as a wife, was so important that the law required the couple to know where the document was at all times. If it was lost, they were required by law to replace it.

If Mary agreed to the terms of the ketubah, the couple would sign it in front of two witnesses, legally binding them as husband and wife. Mary would remain in her father's home for another year while Joseph built an addition on his family complex for them to live as husband and wife. When he and Mary both felt they were ready to consummate the marriage, he and the wedding procession would joyfully escort her from her home to his. Their friends and family would celebrate with them in a wedding feast that lasted for as long as two weeks.

Joseph turned the corner and Mary's home was before him. Her father stood in the doorway to the courtyard, smiling widely.

"Welcome! Come in!"

Joseph stepped across the threshold and found that Mary was already there as well. She smiled shyly as Joseph spread the ketubah across a nearby table for her to review. Joseph fidgeted with his bridal gift as she read, absentmindedly fraying the cord that cinched the bag closed. At last, Mary looked up from the ketubah to the witnesses.

"I agree to these terms," she said. Joseph sighed audibly with relief and Mary laughed.

Mary's father shouted for joy and pulled Joseph into his arms. A moment later the courtyard filled with Mary's mothers, sisters, aunts, uncles, and cousins. Soon the table was piled high with food and wine for the betrothal feast.

Joseph sat beside Mary as dishes were passed and goblets were filled and then emptied again. When the evening finally drew to a close, Joseph walked home through the darkened streets dreaming of the future, the ketubah grasped tightly in his hand. He would have a copy made of it and present it to Mary on the evening of their wedding celebration.

When he arrived home, he stood before his family home under the moonlight. Tomorrow, he would begin preparing a place for his bride.

And when it was perfect, he would bring Mary home.

Father,

Sometimes, in our anticipation of You, we forget Mary and Joseph. We disregard all they gave and sacrificed to play their irreplaceable part in Your redemption of us. They were so young. Surely they had dreams and plans that evaporated like the morning mist so that Your far grander dream might be realized.

Thank You for the gifts of Your servants Mary and Joseph. As I remember them this Advent, nurture in me a willingness to abandon my most cherished dreams and carefully constructed plans when You call me to something bigger and more beautiful than I could ever imagine.

Amen

Fourteen and Pregnant

ZECHARIAH
& ELIZABETH

MARY

ELIZABETH

THEREFORE THE LORD HIMSELF
WILL GIVE YOU A SIGN:
THE VIRGIN WILL CONCEIVE AND
GIVE BIRTH TO A SON,
AND WILL CALL HIM IMMANUEL.
ISAIAH 7:14

Immanuel—God is with us.

Mary sat against the rough, gnarled trunk of an ancient olive tree and gazed out across the terraced hillside. Far below, Nazareth lay nestled in the valley. Her eyes tenderly rested on each of the stone homes filled with treasured family and friends. In the center of Nazareth, rising above all else, was the jewel of her devout hometown: the synagogue.

Mary's earliest and sweetest childhood memories were set in the lofty interior of that holy place. Each Sabbath she sat snuggled close to her mother on one of the benches that lined the walls. The hazan, the synagogue ruler, handed the scroll to the rabbi seated in the center of the room. Then the rabbi unrolled the scroll and began to read, filling the synagogue with the sweet stories of God's great acts of mercy for Israel and His steadfast promises of future rescue.

The readings from Isaiah were always especially poignant. Mary heard them over and over again until they were imprinted upon her mind and heart.

Until they shaped the course of her life.

For to us a child is born, to us a son is given;
and the government will be on His shoulders.
And He will be called Wonderful Counselor, Mighty God,
Everlasting Father, Prince of Peace.
Of the greatness of His government and peace there will be no end.
He will reign on David's throne and over his kingdom,
establishing and upholding it with justice and righteousness
from that time on and forever. (Isaiah 9:6–7)

For centuries, Mary's people told the story of a Messiah who would come to save Israel. The promise became a part of the very fabric of Mary's life. But how could she have ever imagined that God would choose her to be part of His plan for the Messiah?

Mary shook her head in a vain attempt to clear it. Then she stood to walk beneath the olive tree branches as she replayed the morning's events moment by moment. She was sitting in the courtyard of her home alone, spinning wool into yarn, when a stranger stepped across the threshold to greet her.

"Greetings, you who are highly favored! The Lord is with you" (Luke 1:28).

With dreadful surety, Mary knew the stranger was no man but a servant of God. She dropped her work and stood to her feet, her legs shaking beneath her in terror. When the angel spoke again, his voice was gentle and full of compassion.

"Do not be afraid, Mary; you have found favor with God. You will conceive and give birth to a son, and you are to call Him Jesus. He will be great and will be called the Son of the Most High. The Lord God will give Him the throne of His father David, and He will reign over Jacob's descendants forever; His kingdom will never end" (1:30–33).

"How will this be," she had asked the angel, "since I am a virgin?" (1:34).

"The Holy Spirit will come on you, and the power of the Most High will overshadow you. So the holy one to be born will be called the Son of God," the angel explained (1:35).

Mary could only stare at him in stunned silence.

The angel looked at her for a moment and then added earnestly, "Even Elizabeth your relative is going to have a child in her old age, and she who was said to be unable to conceive is in her sixth month. For no word from God will ever fail" (1:37).

And Mary knew it was true. All her life she had heard the stories of God doing the impossible. Around the hearth on long winter nights, her parents told her how the walls of Jericho fell before Joshua at the sound of the priests' trumpet blasts. Each Passover as their family reclined around the table feasting on roasted lamb, unleavened bread, and bitter herbs, her parents told the story of how God delivered His people from Egypt. Mary's God was a God who parted the Red Sea and rained manna from heaven to feed His people. He was a God who led them by cloud and by fire, the great Master of the universe.

Nothing was too hard for God. If God called Mary to serve Him, how could she ever refuse, no matter the cost?

"I am the Lord's servant," she said to the angel. "May your word to me be fulfilled" (1:38).

And then the angel was gone.

Mary wandered over to the olive press and stood before the heavy stone wheel, at rest on its stone base. She placed one hand on her stomach where the angel said a miracle was already underway and then bent down to pick up a few stray olives that had missed the crushing weight of the stone.

Would this miracle crush her, crush Joseph, like the tender olives beneath the wheel? Joseph would know the baby was not his. He would divorce her, of course. A scribe would be hired to declare her offense publicly. She and her sweet father would be shamed. What would her parents say when they found out she was carrying a child before she had consummated her marriage to Joseph?

What would she do? Where would she go? No man of any worth would ever marry her. Everyone would know her story, her child's story.

The other children would call him names.

With terrible finality, Mary saw her cherished future with Joseph swept away. This...would break his kind heart.

Mary knelt beside the olive press, rested her forehead against the rough stone of the base, and turned her heart to the God of the impossible.

"I am Your servant," she whispered through her tears. "May it be to me as You have said."

Immanuel,

During this season of joy and expectation, Your story challenges me to remember that the curse of sin and death was broken at great price.

It cost the Father His Son.

It cost the Son His life.

And it cost Your servants Mary and Joseph too. In obedience to Your call, they laid their future, their reputations, their very lives at Your feet. I am in awe of their faith and inspired by their courage. Through the obedience and sacrifice of two peasant teenagers, heaven came to earth.

Your kingdom, O God, advances still. You call me to work alongside You, sometimes at great cost. When those moments come, fill me with Your Spirit so that I, with Mary, might say, "I am Your servant. May it be to me as You have said."

Amen

Visit to Elizabeth

MARY

ELIZABETH

JOSEPH

TWO ARE BETTER THAN ONE,
BECAUSE THEY HAVE A GOOD
RETURN FOR THEIR LABOR:
IF EITHER OF THEM FALLS DOWN,
ONE CAN HELP THE OTHER UP.
BUT PITY ANYONE WHO FALLS
AND HAS NO ONE TO HELP THEM UP.

ECCLESIASTES 4:9–10

Elizabeth sat on the ground, heels tucked beneath her, and kneaded the dough in the bowl in front of her. A strand of gray hair slipped from beneath her head covering and clung to the perspiration running down her temple. After a moment she grimaced, sat up straight, and rubbed her aching lower back. Then she placed one hand under her heavy abdomen to support it and struggled to her feet.

Slowly, she shuffled over to a bench in a shady corner of the yard and plopped down. She closed her eyes for a moment and laid one hand tenderly across her stomach.

"Oooh!" she cried out in surprise, her eyes flying open as the baby suddenly kicked. The old woman patted the place where the tiny foot had struck and she began to laugh. At first she chuckled softly, then louder and louder until tears rolled down her soft and wrinkled cheeks.

When her laughter subsided, she gazed tenderly down at her abdomen, now still and quiet, and shook her head in awe.

How could this be? How could she, Elizabeth, conceive a child in her old age after a lifetime of barrenness?

Elizabeth turned her face to the sky and held her hands to heaven and prayed: "Give thanks to the LORD, for He is good; His love endures forever" (Psalm 106:1)."

A moment later she walked back across the courtyard, bent to pick up the kneading bowl, and carried it to the beehive-shaped oven. The fire she began earlier that morning had burned down to coals, heating the fragments of pottery that lined the walls of the oven. Expertly, she plucked a portion of dough, rolled it between her palms, flattened it, and then tossed it through the opening where it stuck onto the wall inside. The bread baked quickly. Soon the kneading bowl was empty and a large platter nearby was piled high with fragrant discs of bread.

Elizabeth picked up the platter and gratefully made her way across the yard to the cool interior of her home. A short time later, she sat mending a tear in one of Zechariah's robes when she heard a familiar voice call out in greeting.

"Elizabeth!"

Her cousin Mary stepped through the door. Immediately the baby in Elizabeth's womb began to leap for joy and Elizabeth was filled with the Holy Spirit. She stood and began to prophesy loudly as she crossed the room to Mary.

"Blessed are you among women, and blessed is the child you will bear!" Elizabeth said. "But why am I so favored, that the mother of my Lord should come to me? As soon as the sound of your greeting reached my ears, the baby in my womb leaped for joy. Blessed is she who has believed that the Lord would fulfill His promises to her!" (Luke 1:42–45).

Mary's eyes filled with tears of happiness. She stepped forward and placed one hand on each side of Elizabeth's abdomen. The baby rolled and kicked at her touch.

Life. Elizabeth's long-barren womb was filled with miraculous, abundant life. The angel's words came back to Mary, driving away all doubt and fear: "For nothing will be impossible with God" (Luke 1:37 ESV).

Mary didn't understand how she, a virgin, could conceive the child the angel promised. She didn't know how she would avoid the shame and protentional punishment that accompanied unwed mothers in her culture. Mary had no idea how she would provide for herself and for the child in the long years to come.

But it wasn't her job to know. It was God's.

He only asked that she trust Him moment by moment, day by day. Deep inside Mary's heart, a knot of anxiety and fear untangled as she released everything into God's hands. She took Elizabeth by the hand and led her back to her seat. Then Mary sat on the floor beside her and laid her head against Elizabeth's knee as tears of relief and surrender flowed down her cheeks. Gently, Elizabeth stroked Mary's hair, as the young girl lifted her praises to God:

"My soul glorifies the Lord
and my spirit rejoices in God my Savior,
for He has been mindful
of the humble state of His servant.
From now on all generations will call me blessed,
for the Mighty One has done great things for me—
holy is His name.
His mercy extends to those who fear Him,
from generation to generation.
He has performed mighty deeds with His arm;
He has scattered those who are proud in their inmost thoughts.
He has brought down rulers from their thrones
but has lifted up the humble.
He has filled the hungry with good things
but has sent the rich away empty.
He has helped His servant Israel,
remembering to be merciful
to Abraham and His descendants forever,
just as He promised our ancestors" (1:46–55).

Father,

Thank You for Elizabeth. When young Mary was afraid and needed support, Elizabeth spoke blessing and comfort into her life. Give me godly friends who strengthen my faith in the moments when Your call seems too difficult and the road before me feels too steep.

Empower me, Holy Spirit, to speak words of courage, life, and faith over my brothers and sisters. May we, together, not only celebrate Your Advent with joy but strengthen each other as we work to further Your good and just kingdom on this earth.

Amen

Joseph the Just

ELIZABETH

JOSEPH

MARY

HE HAS TOLD YOU, O MAN, WHAT IS GOOD;
AND WHAT DOES THE LORD REQUIRE OF YOU
BUT TO DO JUSTICE, TO LOVE KINDNESS,
AND TO WALK HUMBLY WITH YOUR GOD?

MICAH 6:8 NASB

S crittch...

Joseph lightly pushed the blade of his hand plane across the piece of cypress on his workbench. A long, thin piece of wood curled up on top of the plane and fell to join the pile of wood chips on the floor. He picked up the cypress piece, held it at eye level to examine it, then blew a fine coat of wood dust from the surface.

Slowly, gently, he ran a calloused hand across the carefully crafted piece. It was a wall shelf, one of the finishing touches for his near-complete home with Mary. A home he no longer needed...

Joseph set down the shelf, braced his hands on the workbench, and closed his eyes, trying and failing to absorb the morning's shocking news: Mary, his betrothed wife, was pregnant. It would have been scandalous enough if the baby had been his, but it wasn't. He had no idea who the father was.

Joseph began to pace angrily back and forth across the room between shelves piled high with tools on one side and a row of projects neatly stacked against the opposite wall of his carpentry shop.

Mary was from a devout family, just like his. He had known her since they were children. She was honest, courageous, and strong. And Mary was smart. She knew the consequences of adultery for both her and her family: They would be ostracized and shamed. The Sanhedrin would order Mary's head shaved as a sign of her disgrace. She might even be stoned to death.

As much as he tried, Joseph could not reconcile the girl he knew and loved with the devastating news she had given him that morning with her grief-stricken father at her side. Three words. It had only taken three words to break his heart and leave his future in ashes...

Joseph, I'm pregnant.

Now, instead of planning a wedding feast, Joseph would begin the painful process of planning a divorce. Although Mary had yet to leave her father's home to live with him, the betrothal process legally bound them as husband and wife. Of course, Joseph could not go forward with the marriage. If he did not divorce Mary, everyone would assume the baby was his. Her sexual immorality would become his scandal as well in the eyes of their community.

Joseph stood in the open doorway and looked across the street where a group of children chased each other beneath the shade of a tall sycamore fig tree. He, Mary, their cousins, and friends had all played beneath that tree as children. He had always assumed their children would play there too.

He sighed, closed his eyes again, and saw Mary's face as she gave him the news of her pregnancy. Her eyes were wide with fear and brimming with tears. Her face was pale with exhaustion.

He imagined her, so young and vulnerable, facing the shame of a public divorce, and slowly his anger began to subside. There would be nowhere for her to hide in their small town. A scribe would march through the narrow streets and loudly announce the divorce and her sin of adultery for all to hear.

Joseph then remembered the words of the Lord as proclaimed by the prophet Isaiah. They were a gift from the long hours he spent memorizing the Torah as a boy at his rabbi's feet.

> Here is My servant, whom I uphold,
> My chosen one in whom I delight;
> I will put my Spirit on Him,
> and He will bring justice to the nations.
> He will not shout or cry out,
> or raise His voice in the streets.
> A bruised reed He will not break,
> and a smoldering wick He will not snuff out.
> In faithfulness He will bring forth justice.
> (Isaiah 42:1–3)

Joseph walked over to an oil lamp neatly tucked into a niche in the wall. The clay lamp was in the shape of a shallow bowl with a delicate spout molded into the rim. An oil-soaked wick trailed over the edge. On a nearby table, a sharpened reed rested against a small pot of ink. Both the wick and the reed were symbols of Isaiah's prophecy. If the wick began to smolder, Joseph knew he would need to snuff it out before it became a fire hazard. If the reed became bruised, and therefore useless for writing, he would snap it in two, toss it into the fire, and get another one. Anyone would.

Anyone but God.

This was Isaiah's message in the metaphor: God is outrageously, *unreasonably* merciful. His definition of justice is not one of crime and punishment. It is to show mercy to the wounded, the vulnerable, and the exhausted.[2]

Joseph picked up a broom leaning against the doorframe and swept the shavings outside. Then he locked the door and began his walk home. His heart was still heavy, but now his mind was clear.

He would divorce Mary quietly. He would not subject her and her family to the scorn of their community. More importantly, Joseph would do everything in his power to save the life of Mary and her unborn child.

That evening, when the lamp was extinguished, Joseph sank into the comfort of his sleeping mat. His body, and his heart, were weary. Silent tears slipped down his cheeks as he mourned for Mary. Gradually, he drifted off to sleep to the comforting rhythm of his parents' breathing and the rustle of the animals in the manger beneath the main room of his home.

As Joseph slept, an angel of the Lord came to him in his dreams. "Joseph son of David, do not be afraid to take Mary home as your

---

[2] Bailey, Kenneth E., *Jesus Through Middle Eastern Eyes* (Downers Grove, IL: IVP Academic, 2008), 44.

wife, because what is conceived in her is from the Holy Spirit. She will give birth to a son, and you are to give Him the name Jesus, because He will save His people from their sins" (Matthew 1:20–21).

At dawn, the sun streamed through the narrow windows at the top of the wall, and Joseph sat up on his mat. Last night's grief had been swept away by the angel's message, making a new space for joy. It was a new day, and Joseph had a new purpose: it was time to bring his wife home.

Water dripped from Joseph's freshly washed hair onto the shoulders of his best tunic. It was early evening as he glanced around the torchlit yard of his family compound where tables were piled high with food. A long row of amphora filled with wine lined one of the rock walls.

His groomsmen gathered around him and began to clap and sing. Joseph smiled and then led the way out through the gate and down the street. The wedding party arrived at Mary's home just as the first stars pierced the night sky. Her father was waiting for them at the gate, his eyes filled with joyful tears.

"I am here to take my wife home," Joseph said to his father-in-law.

Mary's father stepped aside to allow his daughter to step forward and take Joseph's hand. Mary's head was covered with the bridal veil, showing a hint of her long, dark, loose hair. Hand in hand, the couple walked to Joseph's home. The singing groomsmen, now accompanied by Mary's family, followed. As the wedding party made their way through the streets of Nazareth, the procession grew as neighbors rushed from their homes, lamps and flowers in their hands, to join the celebration.

When Mary and Joseph entered the gate of his family compound, they found it filled with more of their friends, neighbors, and large, extended families. The crowd shouted in joy at the sight of the couple and then fell silent in expectation as the rabbi stepped forward to address Joseph.

"Take her according to the law of Moses and of Israel," he said.

At that, the groomsmen stepped forward to place a crown of flowers on both bride and groom. Mary and Joseph were then led to a lamplit table where they each signed their names to the ketubah. At last, the groomsmen led the couple to a quiet corner of the compound where Joseph had built their home. Then, the couple was left to spend some time alone while their friends and families began the weeklong wedding feast.

Once the front door was closed securely behind them, Joseph lifted Mary's veil and took her into his arms. After a moment, the couple parted. Joseph smiled at his bride and handed her the ketubah. Mary blinked back joyful tears as she turned to look around at her new home for the perfect place to keep the precious document secure. At last her eyes rested on a wall shelf, carefully crafted from cypress wood. She crossed the room to it and tenderly ran her fingers across the smooth surface. For a moment she looked down at the ketubah in her hand filled with Joseph's promises to her: He would provide for her, protect her, and care for her. He promised to treat her with dignity always.

Mary closed her eyes and whispered a prayer of thanksgiving as tears slipped past her thick lashes and spilled down her cheeks. Then she opened her eyes, took a deep breath, and placed the ketubah on the shelf Joseph made.

She was home.

Father,

    You give mercy to the wounded and grace to the exhausted. You shelter the vulnerable and defend the weak. When my heart is broken and I feel lost and alone, draw me near. Whisper sweet truth over me and silence my fears.

    I am Yours...
    I am Yours...
    I am Yours...

Amen

Census

JOURNEY *to* BETHLEHEM

ELIZABETH

JOSEPH

MARY

OF THE GREATNESS OF
HIS GOVERNMENT AND PEACE
THERE WILL BE NO END.
HE WILL REIGN ON DAVID'S THRONE
AND OVER HIS KINGDOM,
ESTABLISHING AND UPHOLDING IT
WITH JUSTICE AND RIGHTEOUSNESS
FROM THAT TIME ON AND FOREVER.
THE ZEAL OF THE LORD ALMIGHTY
WILL ACCOMPLISH THIS.

ISAIAH 9:7

C ensus…"

"Slavery…"

"A people for God alone!"

Snippets of the angry conversation reached Joseph as he walked to his carpentry shop. A group of men shouted and gestured wildly as they stood before the steps of the synagogue. Joseph sighed and crossed the street. He had neither time nor energy to get swept up in the heated conversation.

For weeks, the entire country had teetered on the brink of revolt following the announcement of a Roman census. Not only did the census mean increased taxes, it was an assault on everything Israel held dear about her identity: a people who belonged to God alone.

A new sect, the Zealots, had risen in opposition to the census and Roman occupation. The Zealots, who were militant, believed in the defense of Jewish independence at any cost. Their leaders railed against the upcoming census as a precursor to outright slavery. One group of Zealots, the Sicarii, began spreading terror and unrest by carrying long daggers in the sleeves of their robes. They'd slip into crowds, mortally wounding Romans and even Jews if they felt they were Roman sympathizers.

The ever-present threat of flogging and crucifixion by the Romans barely contained the rumble of outright revolt. Still, the Romans steadfastly proceeded with the census, demanding that each household return to their town of origin to make a report. Since Joseph was from the royal line of King David, he and his very pregnant wife, Mary, would make the long trip from Nazareth to Bethlehem. Joseph had family there, and he and Mary would stay with them. The family compound promised to be filled to overflowing as relatives from all over Israel returned to Bethlehem.

Joseph winced as he imagined Mary making the long journey so late in her pregnancy. Still, they had little choice.

The mighty empire of Rome was strengthening its iron grip around Palestine. The populace could revolt and the Zealots could continue their campaign of terror, but it would take a divine act of retribution to deliver the children of Abraham from the world's current superpower.

Israel needed far more than a rebellion. She needed a Messiah.

———————————

"Oh," Mary moaned softly.

Joseph anxiously turned to his wife, trailing along behind him on the back of their donkey. Her face was drawn, her eyes weary from four long days of travel.

"Do you want to walk for a while?" he asked her.

"Yes, thank you."

Joseph held the donkey with one hand while he helped Mary to the ground with the other. Other members of their caravan of extended family plodded steadily past, anxious to make it through the gates of Bethlehem before nightfall.

"We are almost there," he said reassuringly.

Mary nodded, smiling weakly.

Within the hour, the walls of Bethlehem appeared as a long line severing the horizon. The promise of a meal and sleeping mat in the comfort of a relative's home cheered them and they quickened their pace.

Mary and Joseph fell into the silent rhythm of the trail, measuring the last mile of the journey one weary step at a time. At last, as the setting sun bathed Bethlehem in soft golden light, the journey was completed. In the fulfillment of thousands of years of prophecy, the long-awaited Messiah was carried through the gates of Bethlehem, sheltered in the womb of a virgin.

Steadily, Joseph led Mary through the familiar streets to the place called home to his aunts, uncles, and cousins. When he and Mary stepped into the courtyard of the family compound, relatives rushed to meet them, excitedly wrapping Joseph in their arms. One of the children took the donkey's rope and led it to a trough of water. Mary momentarily forgot her fatigue as Joseph's aunts joyfully caressed her burgeoning abdomen, each making their own predictions of how much longer it would be until the baby arrived.

Then, the wizened old matriarch of the family stepped forward. She placed one gentle hand on each side of Mary's face and searched her eyes.

"Ah, daughter," she said, sighing. "You are weary. Come, you need rest." Then she placed an arthritic hand on Mary's stomach and nodded solemnly. "It won't be long now, my child."

Mary glanced back over her shoulder to Joseph as she was led to the comfort of a good meal and a soft sleeping mat. She found him smiling at her, the relief evident on his face. She was in good hands.

That night after the evening meal, Mary and Joseph's sleeping mats were joined with the others that lined the main living room of a relative's home since the kataluma*, the guest room of the home, was full. Immediately, Mary fell into an exhausted sleep. Joseph, though weary, lay awake lost in dark thoughts of the census report. It represented so much to Israel, little of it comforting. What kind of world would Jesus grow up in? How would the brutal rule of Rome mark His life?

Joseph sighed in resignation. There was so little within his control. But for tonight, Mary and the baby were safe. His wife would not give birth on the side of the road but in the care of his family. Kind and experienced women would help the baby into the world.

And with that comforting assurance, Joseph finally surrendered to sleep.

Father,

At just the right moment, as the yoke of slavery fell upon Your people once again, You brought Your Son into the world. Israel cried out for a Messiah, a military ruler who would deliver her from cruel Roman oppression.

But You sent her a different kind of Rescuer. Instead of a warrior, You sent her a gentle Prince of Peace. Rather than offer her nationalistic freedom, You gave Your Son to save her from her sins.

This Advent, teach me that Your dreams of deliverance are always so much greater than mine. Help me rest in You, trusting that Your rescue always comes right on time.

Amen

---

* *Kataluma* has been inaccurately translated as "inn" in some translations of the Bible. A kataluma was the traditional guest room of a home in first-century Palestine. Since everyone was returning to their ancestral homes, this room was understandably full when Mary and Joseph arrived at his family's home in Bethlehem. More recent translations of the Bible (see the 2011 New International Version) have corrected this error.

It's Time

JOSEPH   MARY   THE SHEPHERDS

THEREFORE, THE LORD HIMSELF
WILL GIVE YOU A SIGN:
THE VIRGIN WILL CONCEIVE AND
GIVE BIRTH TO A SON,
AND WILL CALL HIM IMMANUEL.

ISAIAH 7:14

WHEN THE FULLNESS OF TIME HAD COME,
GOD SENT FORTH HIS SON,
BORN OF A WOMAN,
BORN UNDER THE LAW,
TO REDEEM THOSE WHO WERE
UNDER THE LAW,
THAT WE MIGHT RECEIVE THE
ADOPTION AS SONS.

GALATIANS 4:4–5 NKJV

M ary couldn't sit still.

With great effort she rose from the low stool in the court-yard where she and the other women were preparing the evening meal. She placed one hand on her lower back and began to pace back and forth. She felt restless, uneasy.

The older women watched her for a moment before casting knowing looks to each other. Mary's baby was ready to make His entrance.

As the family sat in a circle on the floor, tearing off pieces of pita bread and scooping up couscous and yogurt from the large commu-nal bowl, Mary sat looking at the piece of bread in her hand.

She knew she should be ravenous, but somehow she couldn't eat. She reached up to wipe a trickle of sweat from her temple. The packed room was stifling despite the fact that the sun had set long ago.

A moment later Mary gasped as the dull ache in her lower ab-domen suddenly intensified. One of Joseph's aunts, seated next to her, frowned, reached out to place a hand on her stomach, and found the muscles clenched tight.

"It's time," she said.

Joseph leapt to his feet, his face white with alarm. His uncle chuckled, patted him on the shoulder, and sent him off to get the town midwife. As two of the women helped Mary to her feet, the matriarch of the family began barking orders to the rest of the clan. Normally Mary would have been offered the privacy and comfort of the kataluma, the guest room, but since the house was full of guests and her labor could possibly stretch into the early hours of the morning, they would need to improvise.

Quickly, the animals were evicted from the stables beneath the main living area. The children were tasked with sweeping the area clean and placing fresh straw on the floor. By the time the midwife arrived, Mary was leaning against the cool stone wall of the stables as she waited for the next contraction to pass.

The jovial older woman shuffled into the stables, birthing stool hooked over her arm. Joseph peeked anxiously through the doorway at his wife for a moment before one of the women shooed him away to wait upstairs.

The moment his foot landed on the first step leading to the main living room, Mary cried out in pain. Joseph froze. Beside him, his uncle laid a comforting hand on his shoulder.

"Come, Joseph," he said. "She is in good hands."

Hours later, in the dark early hours of the morning, Mary gasped for air and cried out in pain from the birthing stool, where she leaned back into the supportive arms of Joseph's aunt. The midwife crouched low in front of her, murmuring encouragement.

"It is time to push, my daughter," she said. "Be strong now."

The next contraction tore through Mary's body only seconds after the last one subsided. Then, with a cry of agony, she bore down with all of her remaining strength.

The pain faded as her baby's first cry pierced the night.

"You have a son!" the midwife announced. Upstairs, Joseph's ecstatic shout was joined by the joyful celebration of his uncles and cousins.

In the stables below, the midwife tenderly placed the crying baby on His young mother's chest. Tears flowed down Mary's face as she bent to kiss her son's forehead for the first time.

Joseph peeked around the corner of the stables. His aunt turned to wave him into the room. "Come," she said. "Come meet your son."

Joseph rushed to Mary's side and knelt down to wrap an arm around her. Gently he placed a calloused hand on the baby's head as he blinked back tears of joy.

"Have you chosen a name?" his aunt asked.

"Yeshua," Mary said as she gazed tenderly into the eyes of her son, now quiet and alert. "Yeshua…"

"She will give birth to a son, and you are to give Him the name Jesus [Yeshua], because He will save His people from their sins" (Matthew 1:21).

Father,

When the moment was right, You brought Your Son into the world. The King of all creation, robed in brilliant light, exchanged His glory for our humanity with all of its frailties, vulnerabilities, and indignities.

What a wonder is Your salvation! Steadfastly You pursued our redemption across millennia, entrusting flawed men and women to play their part in carrying it ever forward.

Then, when it was time, You came.

You could have harnessed the wind and ridden its back into our midst. You could have fashioned a chariot of pure starlight for Your grand entrance.

But You came in the womb of a virgin peasant girl from a small town.

And I bow in awe of You.

Amen

A Divine Birth Announcement

MARY   THE SHEPHERDS   THE WISE MEN

FOR TO US A CHILD IS BORN,
TO US A SON IS GIVEN,
AND THE GOVERNMENT WILL
BE ON HIS SHOULDERS.
AND HE WILL BE CALLED
WONDERFUL COUNSELOR,
MIGHTY GOD,
EVERLASTING FATHER,
PRINCE OF PEACE.

ISAIAH 9:6

So, is it true, young Judah? Are you going to approach Anna's father about betrothal?" the good-natured old shepherd asked with a twinkle in his eye.

Judah knew Zachariah meant well, but the last thing he wanted was for his hopes concerning Anna to become the center of the campfire discussion. He remained silent and turned to find another branch for the evening fire.

"Ha!" Luke laughed. "Anna? It is never going to happen, friend."

Then the humor drained from his voice as he quietly added, "Her father would never allow her to marry a shepherd. As far as he, and most everyone else, is concerned, we are nothing more than a bunch of thieves. You would do better to choose a bride from one of the daughters of these men here."

The other shepherds voiced their agreement. Judah set his jaw and jabbed the glowing coals in the base of the fire with a long stick.

"I'm not," he said at last.

The men looked at each other quizzically and then back at him.

"Not what?" Zachariah asked.

Judah stared into the glowing embers.

"I am not a thief."

He stood to throw the stick into the flames, then walked away to gaze out over the moonlit field where a large herd of sheep bleated softly. He turned his eyes to the hills surrounding them. Each family had their own sheepfold on those hills—a cave with a rock wall leading out from each side. At night, the sheep were brought in from the fields to the safety of their fold. The shepherd lay down in the gap in the middle of the wall, serving as the door. Any predator or thief who came to harm the sheep would need to go through him first.

But Judah and his friends had no family sheepfold to call their own. They were camped in the fields at night because their sheep were special sheep. Judah was a temple shepherd, and the sheep in his care were Temple sheep, destined for sacrifice. The irony that he was guarding sacrificial sheep was not lost on Judah. Most people he met on the street each day considered shepherds to be more in need of atonement than others. He wanted to believe they were wrong, but with each new assault to his self-worth, it was getting harder and harder.[3]

He scanned the flock with a practiced eye watching for any disturbance, but the warm summer night was calm. The other shepherds settled into a companionable silence as they watched the animals. The only sound in the stillness of the night was the crackle of the fire and the gentle bleating of the sheep.

Suddenly, a blinding light rent the darkness to reveal a man robed in white. He was tall and powerful, and the air around him shimmered with light. Judah and all the other men cried out in alarm and trembled as they fell facedown before him.

Then the angel spoke, and his voice was like the sound of both music and rushing water.

"Do not be afraid," he said. "I bring you good news that will cause great joy for all the people. Today in the town of David a Savior has been born to you; He is the Messiah, the Lord. This will be a sign to you: You will find a baby wrapped in cloths and lying in a manger" (Luke 2:10–12).

Instantly the entire sky was filled with angels lifting their voices in praise to God.

"Glory to God in the highest heaven, and on earth peace to those on whom His favor rests" (2:14).

Then, as suddenly as they had all appeared, the sky was dark again and the night silent. The shepherds turned to each other.

"Messiah has come!" old Zachariah exclaimed.

---

[3] James C. Martin, John A. Beck, and David G. Hansen, *A Visual Guide to Bible Events* (Grand Rapids, MI: Baker Books, 2009), 146–147.

"Let's go to Bethlehem and see the baby!" another man said.

"I don't know," said another. "If Messiah really has come, do you think His parents would want a crowd of shepherds coming to visit?"

Then Judah spoke. "Weren't you listening to what the angel said? The Messiah isn't in a palace. His parents haven't wrapped Him in silks or placed Him in a gilded cradle. They wrapped Him in cloths and placed Him in a manger, just like we do for our own newborns. I don't understand it, but somehow He is like us."

The men sat thoughtfully for a moment as each one absorbed the significance of the fact that, instead of God presenting long-awaited Messiah to the world in the trappings of royalty, He had swathed Him in the raiment of the poor and the despised.

When Zachariah broke the silence, the old shepherd's voice was heavy with emotion. "Let's go," he said.

One by one the men stood, wrapped their cloaks closer around them, and began the short walk to Bethlehem. With each footfall of their sandals they drew closer to Israel's long-awaited hope—a hope as wide as all creation and yet as near as their own broken hearts.

As they neared Bethlehem, the prophet Isaiah's words seemed to come to life, walking alongside them, whispering ancient words of promise.

"For to us a child is born, to us a son is given" (Isaiah 9:6).

A baby swaddled in rags and lying in a manger. King...and peasant. A Messiah come for even the lowliest of men.

My God and King,

You are clothed with shekinah glory and yet You laid it all aside to take the robe of a peasant. You inhabit eternity, and yet You humbled Yourself to be wrapped in the frailty of infant flesh. With the psalmist I cry, "What is mankind that You are mindful of them, human beings that You care for them?" (Psalm 8:4).

I am so glad Your angelic birth announcement was delivered not to the great but to the dregs of society, because that means I have a place at Your table as well. Thank You, my God, for receiving the poor and the lowly, the weak and the despised. Your coming is truly good news for all!

Amen

Just as the Angels Said

MARY   THE SHEPHERDS   THE WISE MEN

WHO HAS BELIEVED OUR MESSAGE
AND TO WHOM HAS THE ARM OF
THE LORD BEEN REVEALED?
HE GREW UP BEFORE HIM LIKE A TENDER SHOOT,
AND LIKE A ROOT OUT OF DRY GROUND.
HE HAD NO BEAUTY OR MAJESTY
TO ATTRACT US TO HIM,
NOTHING IN HIS APPEARANCE THAT
WE SHOULD DESIRE HIM.
HE WAS DESPISED AND REJECTED BY MANKIND,
A MAN OF SUFFERING, AND FAMILIAR WITH PAIN.
LIKE ONE FROM WHOM PEOPLE HIDE THEIR FACES
HE WAS DESPISED, AND WE HELD HIM IN LOW ESTEEM.

ISAIAH 53:1–3

THE WORD OF THE LORD IS RIGHT AND TRUE;
HE IS FAITHFUL IN ALL HE DOES.

PSALM 33:4

The rising sun breached the horizon behind the shepherds. The walls of Bethlehem were bathed in pale, silvery light. The men quickly made their way inside the city, then paused with uncertainty. The streets were as familiar to them as the rooms of their own homes, but which house held the Messiah?

They clustered together for a moment, trying to remember which families were expecting babies. Just then the midwife, her birthing stool hooked over her arm, rounded the corner.

"Ah!" Zachariah said with delight. "Do we have a new baby in Bethlehem?"

"We do!" she responded. "Young Joseph's wife, Mary, gave birth to their first child just a few hours ago. A son!"

"Of course!" Judah exclaimed. "They came to town for the census. The wife was due to deliver a baby at any time."

A few minutes later, the shepherds stood before Joseph's family compound. Zachariah stepped forward and called into the courtyard.

"Joseph, son of Jacob!"

A moment later, the door to the home directly across the yard opened and Joseph stepped outside, wincing into the bright morning sunlight.

"Welcome!" the weary young father said as he motioned the shepherds forward. Zachariah led the way across the yard to where Joseph stood waiting for them.

"Joseph, we understand your wife has given birth to a son," he began as the other men hung back nervously.

"Yes!" Joseph said proudly. "He was born just a few hours ago."

Zachariah cleared his throat, took a deep breath, and then explained why he and his friends had come.

"We were in the fields watching the sheep at that same hour," he said. "Suddenly an angel appeared in our midst, his robe shining as brightly as the sun. He said he came to bring us wonderful news that would be a source of joy for all people."

Joseph's eyes grew wide as the old shepherd continued. "The angel said the Messiah had been born right here in Bethlehem! He told us that we would find Him swaddled in cloths like a peasant child and lying in a manger. Then, the sky above us was filled with angels singing praises to God. They sang, 'Glory to God in the highest heaven, and on earth peace to those on whom His favor rests'" (Luke 2:14).

"Is it true, Joseph?" Zachariah asked, his voice breaking. "Has Messiah truly come at last...as one of us?"

Joseph's eyes filled with tears as he remembered his own angelic visitor many months before. The angel's message had changed the young carpenter's life. Joseph smiled and turned to open the door behind him.

"Come and see," he said.

The shepherds gathered in the entryway and paused to allow their eyes to adjust to the dim light inside. Joseph led the way into the stable on the lower level where Mary was resting on fresh straw beside a manger hewn out of stone. Joseph explained to Mary why the shepherds had come to visit. She nodded, her eyes crinkling in a smile above her veil, and motioned for the men to come closer.

Timidly, the shepherds approached the manger. A small bundle was nestled into the straw. The tiny baby's cheeks were round and pink. A dark, feathery swath of hair encircled His head. As they watched, the child began turning His head to the side, stretching His mouth wide in search of His mother's milk.

"What is His name?" Judah asked softly.

"Yeshua," Joseph answered.

"Yeshua...The Lord Saves," Zachariah whispered in awe. "And He is wrapped in cloths like a shepherd's babe..."

The men stood silently for a moment watching the child. Suddenly Judah spoke. "This is a Messiah for everyone, even shepherds like us! It really is 'good news that will bring joy to all the people.' Come! We must tell people!"

With one last glance at the baby in the manger, the men turned to retrace their steps back to the fields, proclaiming the good news of Jesus's birth to everyone they met.

"Messiah has been born at last! An angel appeared to us as we kept watch over our flocks. He said we would find the baby wrapped in cloths and lying in a manger like a peasant child. We have seen it with our own eyes! It was just as the angel said."

Father,

Your Word is flawless, forever faithful and true. At Eden's gate, as exile stretched endlessly before Adam and Eve, You whispered a promise over the dark night of their souls: I will come for you and bring you home.

Your promise of rescue sustained Your people throughout generations. It upholds us still.

I rejoice in the hope of Your Son, the greatest gift of all. With the angels and shepherds, I cry, "Glory to God in the highest!"

Amen

Visitors from the East

ARISE, SHINE, FOR YOUR LIGHT HAS COME,
AND THE GLORY OF THE LORD RISES UPON YOU.
SEE, DARKNESS COVERS THE EARTH
AND THICK DARKNESS IS OVER THE PEOPLES,
BUT THE LORD RISES UPON YOU
AND HIS GLORY APPEARS OVER YOU.
NATIONS WILL COME TO YOUR LIGHT,
AND KINGS TO THE BRIGHTNESS OF YOUR DAWN.
HERDS OF CAMELS WILL COVER YOUR LAND,
YOUNG CAMELS OF MIDIAN AND EPHAH.
AND ALL FROM SHEBA WILL COME,
BEARING GOLD AND INCENSE
AND PROCLAIMING THE PRAISE OF THE LORD.

ISAIAH 60:1–3, 6

Frahāta lifted one hand to shield his eyes from the glare of the setting sun as the other hand held tight to the reins of his camel. He sighed with relief and then turned to one of his heavily armed guards riding horseback alongside him.

"There is an inn ahead," he said. "We will stay there for the night to rest. Tomorrow by midday we will arrive in Jerusalem. Inform the rest of the caravan."

With a call to his mount, the guard turned and rode toward the back of the line of riders, shouting instructions to the other royal emissaries and the warriors guarding them.

"We rest just ahead, and then tomorrow, Jerusalem!" he cried.

Shouts of joy returned his call. Their long journey was almost over. Tomorrow they would finally honor the new King of the Jews on behalf of the Parthian Kingdom. Their mission was almost over.

The caravan reached the safety of the inn just as the sun's last golden rays faded from the horizon. Frahāta dismounted his camel. As one of his guards stood watch, his hand on the hilt of his sword, Frahāta reached into his saddlebag to retrieve an intricately carved box of cypress wood. He turned to look behind him and saw the other two official emissaries, also retrieving precious parcels from their bags as guards stood protectively nearby.

This night, as so many nights before, the three men would sleep with the treasures by their sides for safekeeping.

Gold, frankincense, and myrrh...gifts for the new King.

The rest of the delegation filed slowly into the inn, each claiming his bed for the night as Frahāta and his guard lingered outside for a moment. Frahāta handed the reins of his camel to a servant and turned to look to the southwestern night sky strewn with stars.

One star, however, shone more brightly than all the rest. This star's rising was the reason for their long journey. It had gone before them night after night as they left Parthia and journeyed north along the Euphrates River. Eventually it led them west across the northern border of Arabia and west into Palestine. This night it shone brighter than ever before as it hung low in the southern sky over Jerusalem.

They were almost there.

Frahāta slowly dismounted his camel, never taking his eyes off the Roman guards standing between him and the gates of Jerusalem.

"We are here as official representatives of the government of Parthia," Frahāta said as he cautiously extended a scroll toward the soldier who appeared to be the leader. The guard unrolled the scroll and scanned it before handing it back to Frahāta.

"Where is the one who has been born King of the Jews?" he asked the guard. "We saw His star when it rose and have come to worship Him" (Matthew 2:2).

With that, the large crowd of people who had gathered to gawk at the strangers gasped and then began to whisper anxiously to each other. King Herod the Great had become increasingly paranoid in his old age, even to the point of killing his own sons because he feared they posed a threat to his throne. At one point he became convinced his favorite wife, Mariamne, was plotting against him and ordered her execution. He now spent his days crying out for his servants to bring her to him and then beating them when they failed to do so.

What would he do when he discovered his old enemies, the Parthians, had arrived asking for the "new King of the Jews"?

The Roman guards took a moment to discuss the situation while warily watching the group of strangers. Three richly robed noblemen wearing long, V-necked tunics belted at the waist over loose trousers sat stoically atop the multicolored cloth saddles of their camels. Surrounding them were heavily armed, burly warriors on horseback.

At last it was decided that the issue was an internal one for the Jews and their reigning king, Herod. The lead guard stepped forward and pointed to three ornate towers rising above the city—the palace of Herod.

Frahāta, Hmayeak, and Rta-pāna[4] walked slowly and cautiously toward the end of the columned throne room where Herod sat waiting for them.

When they drew near, Herod shifted his ponderous frame and winced in pain. He was frighteningly pale. Thin beads of sweat lined his forehead and trickled down his temples.

"Welcome, friends," he said, panting for breath. "Tell me, when did the star you are following first appear?"

"It first rose almost two years ago, giving us time to make the long journey for His birth," Frahāta said, bowing slightly.

"Yes, yes…," Herod said as he absentmindedly scratched his arm until the skin turned blotchy and red. Then he smiled benevolently. "Go and search carefully for the child. As soon as you find Him, report to me, so that I too may go and worship Him" (2:8).

The three men bowed before the king and turned to leave. By the time Frahāta, Hmayeak, and Rta-pāna rejoined their guards outside the palace walls, daylight was fading quickly. The guards began to close the gates for the night as the last of the caravan left Jerusalem. Before them, the star shone brightly in the sky, urging them ever onward.

Less than two hours later, the star stood still over the home of

---

4 Author's note: We don't know the names of the wise men. These names were chosen from Parthian names discovered in historical writings from the first century for documentation. To see the meanings of the names, go to http://www.iranica-online.org/articles/personal-names-iranian-iv-parthian.

peasants in the tiny town of Bethlehem. Frahāta shook his head in disbelief as he stood peering down from the back of his camel at the modest cluster of homes around a center yard of what was clearly a family compound. He glanced up at the night sky to find the star securely fixed above the modest dwellings.

This was the home of the King of the Jews?

He turned to smile at Hmayeak and Rta-pāna, who laughed in disbelief before dropping to the ground beside their camels. Frahāta dismounted and the three men reached in their saddlebags to retrieve their treasures.

For a moment, they stood silently. They were eager to complete their mission but hesitant to intrude. In each home in the compound, faint lamplight shone through the narrow windows. One home, a bit larger than the others, stood in the center of the yard. They could hear laughter and happy chatter, the familiar sounds of a large family sharing an evening meal.

Then, above it all, the cry of a baby.

Frahāta smiled and knocked at the gate.

The door of the home opened, and several men looked out. One of them, holding a lamp, cautiously led the way across the yard. Once they reached the gate, they stood silently dumbfounded for a moment as they observed the men before them: foreigners wearing strange clothes in rich fabrics.

Frahāta, Hmayeak, and Rta-pāna smiled and bowed low in greeting. "We are here to welcome the child," Frahāta explained.

The other men turned to look at a young man, hardly more than a boy, standing at the back of the group. When he stepped into the lamplight, Frahāta saw that his eyes were thoughtful.

"I am Joseph, the child's father," he said softly as he opened the gate. "Welcome."

Joseph led the way across the yard to the home, opened the door, and called up the stairs.

A moment later, a young girl stepped outside. Her eyes above her veil were questioning but warm. The chubby baby in her arms, His hair a mass of dark curls, tugged at her robe and laughed. She turned Him around and held Him with His back against her chest so that the visitors could see Him.

The baby looked up into Frahāta's eyes, laughed, and then cooed. Frahāta smiled, dropped to his knees before Mary and Jesus, and held his offering high. Hmayeak and Rta-pāna knelt and lifted their gifts to the child as well. "Gifts for the King of the Jews from the king of Parthia," Frahāta said.

Then the three wise men from the East reverently placed their treasures at the feet of a Jewish peasant girl and her infant son, born to be a light to both Jews and Gentiles—the Messiah whose salvation would reach to the very ends of the earth.

Immanuel,
Once we were strangers, lost and far away.
Raging and wounded.
Addicted to violence.
Shackled by sin and shame.
Then You came.
You set the prisoners free,
And satisfied our deepest longings with Your love.
You stilled our hearts and healed our wounds.
You found us.
And then, You brought us home.
Alleluia and amen

Out of Egypt I Called My Son

WHEN ISRAEL WAS A CHILD, I LOVED HIM,
AND OUT OF EGYPT I CALLED MY SON.
BUT THE MORE THEY WERE CALLED,
THE MORE THEY WENT AWAY FROM ME.
THEY SACRIFICED TO THE BAALS
AND THEY BURNED INCENSE TO IMAGES.
IT WAS I WHO TAUGHT EPHRAIM TO WALK,
TAKING THEM BY THE ARMS;
BUT THEY DID NOT REALIZE
IT WAS I WHO HEALED THEM.
I LED THEM WITH CORDS OF HUMAN KINDNESS,
WITH TIES OF LOVE.
TO THEM I WAS LIKE ONE WHO LIFTS
A LITTLE CHILD TO THE CHEEK,
AND I BENT DOWN TO FEED THEM.

HOSEA 11:1–4

G et up."

Joseph tossed fitfully back and forth on his sleeping mat at the angel's sudden appearance in his dream.

"Get up." the angel said. *"Take the child and His mother and escape to Egypt. Stay there until I tell you, for Herod is going to search for the child to kill Him"* (Matthew 2:13).

Joseph's eyes flew open in the darkness, his heart pounding in his chest. He reached past the curly-haired infant sleeping beside him to awaken Mary.

"Mary, Mary!" Joseph whispered as he shook her arm. "Wake up!"

Mary pushed herself up onto her elbow and looked at him with alarm. "Joseph, what's wrong?" she asked sleepily.

"Mary, we have to flee. The Lord just came to me in a dream and told me Herod is going to search for Jesus to kill Him. We have been instructed to go to Egypt until it is safe to return."

Instantly Mary was on her feet. She lit a lamp, pulled a bag from the peg on the wall, and began to pack some food for the trip and clothes for the baby. Joseph hurried across the room and moved a table away from the wall. He knelt on the floor and ran his hands along the stones in the wall in front of him until he located the loose brick. He grasped the edges with his fingers, wiggled it, and pulled it loose. He reached inside the opening and removed a bag of gold, a box of frankincense, and a jar of myrrh. These gifts the men from the East had brought only days before would fund their journey.

Joseph placed the treasures into his bag and took Mary's parcels from her. She bent down and scooped Jesus into her arms. He instinctively snuggled into the curve of her neck and pushed His thumb into His mouth without ever awakening. Joseph smiled sadly at his son and reached to tenderly stroke His curls.

"We have to go," he said to Mary.

She blinked back tears and nodded her assent. They walked down the stairs to the stable below. Joseph slipped a rope around the donkey's neck and led it outside as Mary and Jesus followed.

Bethlehem was silent under the moonlight. Joseph helped his wife and son onto the donkey and tied the bags onto its back. Then Joseph grasped the rope and began to walk away from all he had ever known...

Egypt. It seemed a bit ironic that the country synonymous with Israel's slavery would shelter her Redeemer. But there was infinite wisdom in God's plan. Egypt was nearby, and Herod would never risk pursuing the Christ child too far within the borders of that land.

Years before, Herod's superior, Mark Antony, had been consumed with passion for Egypt's queen, Cleopatra VII. She was consumed by passion as well, but hers was a passion for power.

One of Cleopatra's greatest desires was to dominate and destroy Herod the Great. She relentlessly tried to convince her lover to give her Herod's kingdom. In 35 BC, Mark Antony relented and transferred large tracts of Palestine to Cleopatra.

But just five years later, their love affair came to a dramatic end with their suicides, and Herod took the opportunity to bring his lost territories back under his control. However, even after their deaths, the powerful legacy left behind by Cleopatra and Mark Antony still served to limit Herod's reach.

Egypt was a good hiding place for another reason as well. When the priesthood in Jerusalem became corrupt under Roman rule, members of the true, Zadokite priestly line fled to Egypt to find protection under Ptolemaic rule. They built a city there and named it Leontopolis, the "city of lions." The Jewish priest Onias received the Ptolemies' blessing to build a temple to Jehovah. It was the only Jewish sanctuary outside of Jerusalem where sacrifices were offered. This community of observant Jews would open their arms to the young family and shelter them until the threat of Herod had passed...

The road before Joseph and Mary stretched dark and lonely into the night as they left Bethlehem behind. Then somewhere in the distance, they heard crashes, shouts, and—above it all—a mournful wail piercing the night. The wail was joined by another and another, growing and growing as an ancient prophecy was fulfilled. In his determination to kill Jesus, Herod had ordered his soldiers to slaughter all of Bethlehem's baby boys under the age of two.

Joseph grasped the rope tighter and quickened his pace. Mary clutched her baby boy to her chest and buried her face into His hair to muffle her sobs.

And Jesus slept. God's Son, the Infinite One, was wrapped in vulnerability and nestled in the arms of a young girl. He would go to Egypt, and when the time was right, God would call His Son back to the land of Israel to fulfill His divine and eternal purpose. Jesus would then walk among His people, point the way to the kingdom of God, and then allow Himself to be led like a lamb to the slaughter for the redemption of all mankind.

My Redeemer,

You have witnessed every act of brutality throughout the course of human history. Who could have blamed You if You considered us a lost cause? But You didn't. You redeemed our savagery when You allowed it to wash over You in its fullness on the cross.

Sometimes, Jesus, the atrocities human beings inflict on one another take my breath away. Help me remember that the world You were born into and died at the hands of was brutal as well.[5]

But on the third day, You rose from the grave. Someday, when You return, man will make war no more.

Come quickly, Lord Jesus.

Amen

---

[5] Bailey, Kenneth E., *Jesus Through Middle Eastern Eyes* (Downers Grove, IL: IVP Academic, 2008), 58.

Baby's First Trip to the Temple

JOSEPH, MARY, & JESUS

SIMEON

JOSEPH, MARY, & JESUS

THE LORD SAID TO MOSES, "CONSECRATE
TO ME EVERY FIRSTBORN MALE. THE
FIRST OFFSPRING OF EVERY WOMB
AMONG THE ISRAELITES BELONGS TO
ME, WHETHER HUMAN OR ANIMAL."
THEN MOSES SAID TO THE PEOPLE,
"COMMEMORATE THIS DAY, THE DAY YOU
CAME OUT OF EGYPT, OUT OF THE LAND
OF SLAVERY, BECAUSE THE LORD BROUGHT
YOU OUT OF IT WITH A MIGHTY HAND."
Exodus 13:1–3

THE FIRST OFFSPRING OF EVERY WOMB
BELONGS TO ME, INCLUDING ALL THE
FIRSTBORN MALES OF YOUR LIVESTOCK,
WHETHER FROM HERD OR FLOCK....
REDEEM ALL YOUR FIRSTBORN SONS.
NO ONE IS TO APPEAR BEFORE
ME EMPTY-HANDED.
Exodus 34:19–20

*S*imeon... Simeon...".

The old man's eyes flew open in the early-morning sun. The Holy Spirit's presence rested heavily upon the room.

"Go to the Temple. It is time."

Simeon's heart leaped with excitement. For years he'd had one fervent desire: to see the coming Messiah. He had watched and waited as kingdoms rose and fell and his body withered with age, but he held fast to hope. The Holy Spirit promised him that he would not die before his longing was fulfilled. Now, the Spirit was calling to him with the joyful news that the time had come.

Simeon placed one hand on the edge of his low bed and pushed himself up to a seated position. Then he grasped his walking stick and struggled to his feet. He took a few slow, stiff steps to his front door and then out into the street. Once there, he paused and gazed into the distance at the temple. It shone like a gemstone as brilliant sunlight reflected off its surface.

Could it really be? After so many years of waiting, had God's promise come true at last?

Simeon grasped his walking stick a little tighter and took the first step up his familiar route to the Temple.

At that very moment a young family was nearing the Temple gates. The father, Joseph, grasped a bag of coins in his hand. There were five shekels of silver for the offering and a bit more to buy the two young doves for the sacrifice. Mary carried her infant son in her arms. He was forty days old, and the time for her ritual purification had drawn to an end. In obedience to the law, they had walked the five miles from Bethlehem to come to the temple for Mary's purification and to complete the rite of the firstborn for Jesus.

Mary and Joseph paused at the southern steps of the temple. Before she could enter the Temple complex, the new mother would need to take a ritual purification bath in the women's mikvah located at the base of the stairs. She handed the baby to Joseph, then ducked inside the cool, lamplit interior of the bath.

A short time later, Mary emerged from the mikvah smiling, her hair still damp. She reached for Jesus as Joseph returned the baby to her arms. Then the family turned to enter the temple through the subterranean staircase of the Huldah Gates. Moments later, they emerged in the sunlit, expansive Court of the Gentiles.

Simeon stood at the base of the southern steps and gazed at the huge, columned gates at the top. The thirty-one steps measured two hundred feet up and seemed steeper every time he came to the temple. But there was a promise waiting for him in the temple courts, and it was most certainly worth climbing those steps one more time. He took a deep breath and began the ascent.

Joseph and Mary found the Court of the Gentiles to be crowded as usual as worshipers jostled to pay their temple taxes and purchase animals for sacrifice. Joseph left Mary and the baby in a shaded alcove and slipped away to purchase doves for the sacrifice. The standard sacrifice for purification was a lamb, but the poor were allowed to offer two young doves or pigeons instead. This was the offering Joseph and Mary would present to the priest. A few moments later, he returned with the two gentle birds in a small cage constructed of sticks and twigs.

The young family moved through the crowd toward the Court of Women. Once there, they climbed the fifteen semicircular steps at the end, which led to the immense bronze Nicanor Gates. Joseph, Mary, and Jesus waited at the top of the steps for the priest on duty to receive their sacrifice and then perform the ceremony for Jesus.

Simeon entered the temple courts and leaned against one of the lofty columns of the colonnade to catch his breath. His hand trembled and his knuckles whitened as he clutched his walking stick. He bowed his head for a moment, then lifted it to gaze across the Court of the Gentiles to the Court of Women beyond. The Nicanor Gates gleamed in the sunlight, and Simeon could see small figures standing at the base of the gates waiting for the priest. His heart began to beat a bit faster and he began walking in that direction, never taking his eyes off of the figures waiting at the top of the stairs.

The priest on duty approached Mary and Joseph. She kissed the baby gently and handed Him to His father. Then she took the doves and gave them to the priest. He left for a moment to perform the sacrifice. When he returned, Mary closed her eyes as he sprinkled her with the blood of the doves and declared her clean.

Next, the priest took the baby in his arms and held Him aloft and began the Rite of the Redemption of the Firstborn, a ceremony of remembrance of God's deliverance of His children from the bondage of Egypt. He began by thanking God for the gift of the newborn child. Next, the priest raised his voice in joyful praise to God for the child's redemption. When the benediction was complete, Mary presented the priest with her offering of five shekels of silver. The priest gently returned the sleeping infant to His mother's arms.

Mary and Joseph beamed at each other and then down at their beautiful baby boy. Then, with hearts filled with gratitude, they began to descend the steps.

But the ceremony wasn't yet complete. There was someone waiting for them at the bottom of the stairs.

Simeon's eyes filled with tears of joy as he watched the ceremony. When Mary and Joseph reached him, his walking stick clattered to the ground as he stretched out trembling arms toward the infant. Mary looked at Joseph, and then into the old man's eyes. She smiled and gently placed her baby in his arms.

Simeon pulled the baby close and wept.

"Sovereign Lord," Simeon prayed through his tears, "as You have promised, You may now dismiss Your servant in peace. For my eyes have seen Your salvation, which You have prepared in the sight of all nations: a light for revelation to the Gentiles, and the glory of Your people Israel" (Luke 2:29–32).

The wait had been long, but God had been faithful, so very faithful. Simeon's every longing was fulfilled.

Faithful God,

You are a God of truth and forever faithful. No matter how dark my path becomes or how long Your deliverance seems to linger, I can rest in Your promises. Help me to trust the wisdom of Your timing and the kindness of Your heart. Give me, O God, the endurance to wait well.

Amen

In My Father's House

SIMEON

JOSEPH, MARY,
& JESUS

AND NOW THE LORD SAYS—
HE WHO FORMED ME IN THE
WOMB TO BE HIS SERVANT
TO BRING JACOB BACK TO HIM
AND GATHER ISRAEL TO HIMSELF,
FOR I AM HONORED IN THE EYES OF THE LORD
AND MY GOD HAS BEEN MY STRENGTH—
HE SAYS:
"IT IS TOO SMALL A THING FOR
YOU TO BE MY SERVANT
TO RESTORE THE TRIBES OF JACOB
AND BRING BACK THOSE OF
ISRAEL I HAVE KEPT.
I WILL ALSO MAKE YOU A LIGHT
FOR THE GENTILES,
THAT MY SALVATION MAY REACH
TO THE ENDS OF THE EARTH."

ISAIAH 49:5–6

The sun sank low on the horizon, signaling to the caravan of Passover pilgrims that it was time to stop for the night. The men had traveled in one group, the women and children in another; but once the day's journey drew to a close, it was time for families to reunite.

Joseph was busy getting the fire started when he saw Mary walking his way. He smiled, stood, and brushed the dust off his hands. As she drew nearer, he noticed her face was creased with worry.

"What's wrong?" he asked her.

"I can't find Jesus," she said.

"I am sure He is here somewhere," Joseph said. "He is probably off with the other boys."

He gave her a reassuring smile and took her hand in his.

"Let's go," he said. "I will help you look."

Long evening shadows fell as they walked from campsite to campsite, asking if any of their relatives or friends had seen Jesus. Time and again, the answer was no. In fact, no one remembered seeing Him all day. With each negative response, their anxiety grew and hope faded until at last they were forced to face the unthinkable.

Somehow they had left their son a day's journey behind them in Jerusalem—Israel's largest city.

Darkness had fallen by the time Mary and Joseph returned to their campsite. Joseph collapsed next to the fire and put his head in his hands as Mary paced back and forth.

"We have to go back, Joseph! We have to go find Him!"

Joseph stood wearily and walked over to pull her into his arms.

"We will leave as soon as the sun rises," he said.

Neither of them slept well. As soon as the first hint of sunrise marked the horizon, Joseph and Mary gathered their belongings and poured water over the smoldering campfire. They stepped back on the road to Jerusalem while their family and friends were still asleep. The caravan would return to Nazareth without them.

When they arrived in the city, they found it much quieter than when they had left it. Thousands of pilgrims had returned home, shrinking Jerusalem to her natural size. Their first stop was the home of the friends with whom they had spent Passover. Joseph and Mary hoped Jesus had returned there once He realized the caravan had left without Him, but there had been no sign of Him. Their friends kindly offered them the kataluma, the guest room, for the night. Joseph gratefully accepted before he and Mary left to search Jerusalem for their son.

They walked up and down the streets all day, constantly scanning the crowds. Each time they spotted a boy Jesus's size, their hearts leapt, only to be disappointed when they realized it wasn't Him. At the end of the day, they returned to their friends' home, their spirits as weary as their feet.

That night in the kataluma, Mary lay on her mat facing Joseph as tears ran down her face. He reached out in the darkness to take her hand in his. Then exhaustion claimed them both and they drifted off to sleep.

As soon as morning dawned, they resumed their search. They scoured markets, alleyways, and even the crowded Pool of Bethesda, where the diseased and lame waited for the healing waters to stir.

But night fell once again, and still their son was lost.

On the third day, Joseph and Mary wearily took to the streets again. This time, they made their way to the highest point in Jerusalem—the temple. They stood before the southern steps and looked up at the massive gates at the top. The thirty-one steps—some wide, some narrow—were purposely designed to be irregular to force those who entered the temple to slow their pace and enter God's house thoughtfully. With heavy hearts, Mary and Joseph began their ascent.

Once at the top, they paused and gazed at the surrounding

landscape, searching for Jesus, but they didn't see Him anywhere. After a moment, they turned and entered the temple courts. They looked past the Roman guards standing watch underneath the col-umned colonnade and scanned the expansive Court of the Gen-tiles. In the center of the complex rose the temple itself. It glittered brilliantly in gold and white in the morning sun as smoke from the sacrifices rose from the altar.

Mary and Joseph passed into the Court of Women, lined with four lofty candelabras. At the end of the court, fifteen semi-circular steps rose to the massive, bronze Nicanor Gates that led into the Court of the Israelites and the temple beyond it. The Court of Women was busy as usual with ceremonies and small groups of men discussing the law. Mary and Joseph stood in the center of it all looking for Jesus, and for a moment it seemed their search had reached a futile end.

Then Mary reached out and placed a hand on Joseph's arm as she tilted her head to one side. She stood listening for a moment before turning toward a group of the teachers of the law sitting to the left. Joseph followed her gaze. One of the men shifted position to reveal the top of a familiar head in the center of the group.

Mary grasped Joseph's arm tighter as her knees gave way with relief. "It's Him!" she whispered.

Joseph closed his eyes and sighed. He squeezed Mary's hand and released it to walk over to the edge of the group. At that moment, a cry of astonishment arose from the teachers of the law in response to one of Jesus's answers.

"Amazing! Who taught this child?"

Jesus looked up to see His father. When their eyes met, the boy smiled. Joseph motioned for his son to come with him. Jesus stood, excused Himself from the men, and joined him.

Joseph led Jesus to Mary, who immediately wrapped Him in her arms and buried her face in the top of His head as she struggled not to cry. Then she held Him at arm's length and looked into His eyes.

"Son, why have you treated us like this? Your father and I have been anxiously searching for You," she said (Luke 2:48).

Jesus frowned and innocently asked, "Why were you searching for Me? Didn't you know I had to be in My Father's house?" (2:49).

Mary and Joseph looked at each other. They were speechless. She pulled Jesus into her arms once again. Joseph reached out and placed a calloused hand on his boy's head and gently tousled His curls. Then the small family turned to leave the glittering temple courts behind and return to the simplicity of village life in Nazareth. It was time to go home.

What seemed like an odd adolescent misstep to Jesus's parents was actually the impeccable timing of a twelve-year-old Redeemer. Hundreds of years before Jesus entered the temple courts built by Herod the Great, the Babylonians defeated the Jews and destroyed another temple—the beloved, magnificent house of worship built by King Solomon. The Israelites were devastated, but God comforted His people with the promise that He would restore them after seventy years. He was faithful to that promise, and the temple was rebuilt 70 years later, just as He said. As a result, the number seventy became synonymous with God's rescue of His people.

When the Romans seized control of Israel in 63 BC, many of the Jewish faithful began the countdown to the year 70 once again. It was a mark they were *just* approaching when Jesus stayed behind at age twelve in "[His] Father's house."

Even as a boy, Jesus was intentional about His purpose. And this was what He attempting to explain to His frightened parents at the very moment when the faithful all over Jerusalem began lifting their eyes from their calendars to look for signs of a deliverer.

Once again, God had been faithful. The Deliverer had come. He was exactly where He *had* to be...in His Father's house.

My Jesus,

When You walked among us, each step You took was in pursuit of Your Father's kingdom and the salvation of all mankind. You were always so intentional in Your redemption of us. I am overwhelmed by Your great love, Your relentless courage… Your heroic heart. How could I help but love You, beautiful Redeemer?

Amen

Conclusion

As Adam and Eve left the Great King's royal garden in Eden, they carried with them not only the consequences of their rebellion but the promise that God would ransom them, and all Creation, from the clutches of sin and death. Like a scarlet ribbon ever unraveling from the Creator's hand, Adam and Eve took the promise of redemption with them into the barren wilderness of exile.

In desperate hope, Adam and Eve held on to God's promise through each new sorrow the sin-cursed earth laid at their feet. Eve bore sons, Cain and Abel, only to lose them both—one to murder, and the other to exile. God mercifully gave her another son, Seth. It was into his hands that she placed the scarlet ribbon, now stained with blood and tears.

Seth passed it on to his son, Enosh, who in turn gifted it to his son. Down through the generations, the ribbon passed...

Abraham carried it with him into Canaan...

His great-great-grandson, Joseph, wound the ribbon through the sands of Egypt...

Moses trailed it through the Wilderness of Zin as he led God's people to the Promised Land...

Naomi pressed it into the outstretched hand of her daughter-in-law Ruth as Ruth went into the fields to glean wheat...

A shepherd boy, David, tied it to his staff as he knelt for Samuel to anoint him king of Israel...

The scarlet ribbon of redemption was carried by ordinary men and women throughout the corridors of history until, at last, it came to rest in a manger in Bethlehem. There, a young Jewish girl, a virgin, draped the ribbon across the palm of her newborn baby. The Son of God's tiny fingers curled around it, clutching it tight as His mother named Him "Jesus," because He would save His people from their sins.

Jesus grew. He carried the ribbon with Him as He played tag in the narrow streets of Nazareth, sat at His rabbi's feet, and trained as a carpenter's apprentice.

He became a man. He healed the sick, raised the dead, and opened the eyes of the blind. He showed grace and mercy to outcasts and spoke hard truths to those in power.

Jesus carried the ribbon all the way to His cross. There he tied it around His hands and feet and wove it into the crown of thorns as He surrendered Himself to the humiliation and agony of Roman crucifixion.

Then, with a loud cry, He proclaimed, "It is finished!" Eden's curse was broken. The ransom was paid in full, opening the door for God's children to come home.

Just as the Creator promised.

"For no word from God will ever fail" (Luke 1:47).

Amen

LIVE YOUR FAITH

Dear Friend,

This book was prayerfully crafted with you, the reader, in mind—every word, every sentence, every page—was thoughtfully written, designed, and packaged to encourage you...right where you are this very moment. At DaySpring, our vision is to see every person experience the life-changing message of God's love. So, as we worked through rough drafts, design changes, edits and details, we prayed for you to deeply experience His unfailing love, indescribable peace, and pure joy. It is our sincere hope that through these Truth-filled pages your heart will be blessed, knowing that God cares about you—your desires and disappointments, your challenges and dreams.

He knows. He cares. He loves you unconditionally.

BLESSINGS!
THE DAYSPRING BOOK TEAM

———————

Additional copies of this book and
other DaySpring titles can be purchased
at fine bookstores everywhere.
Order online at dayspring.com
or
by phone at 1-877-751-4347